Someone Misplaced My Identity: God Can You Help Me?

Charles E. Maldon Sr

ISBN: 978-1-60383-061-4

Published by:
Holy Fire Publishing
Unit 116
1525-D Old Trolley Rd.
Summerville, SC 29485

www.ChristianPublish.com

Cover Design: Jay Cookingham

Printed in the United States of America and the United Kingdom

Acknowledgements

In honor of those slaves and stalwart Black and White freedom fighters who contributed to help Blacks in their search for their identity.

CONTENTS

ONE

INTRODUCTION

It is the year of 2007. Long ago, a dark race of people was forced into slavery on the American Continent. Today, the cruel pain of those chains can no longer be felt physically. But physical pain is not the only form of misery that can destroy a people. Throughout history men have fought for the freedom to rule themselves. But in the 1600s Blacks discovered that their freedom had been taken away. Almost 250 years elapsed before the institution of slavery was finally ruled inhumane. Many of our ancestors died so that we could obtain freedom. And yet today many Blacks consider the struggles of those stalwarts insignificant.

No one can deny that Blacks have made great strides in the business, corporate, entertainment and sports worlds. In fact, Prince Georges (PG) County of Maryland has more high income Blacks than any other county in the United States. But PG County also boasts one of the highest crime rates in the country. While black people in America have a lot to be proud of, they must also recognize the deteriorating conditions facing them as a race and a culture. What happened to the dreams that our black ancestors envisioned? There has been a steady erosion of the strong family values and Christian principles that used to identify the Black race. Some might argue that nothing is wrong, despite the telling statistical data that speaks to the contrary. The spiritual foundation of the Black race has been and will continue to be tested.

Sure enough, racial discrimination continues to have a significant impact on the lives of Blacks. Nevertheless, a greater problem than racial discrimination may be hovering over the heads of black people today. That problem is "self-destruction."

Many Blacks pursue meaningless things that have, over time, destroyed their once proud image. The modern day love of money, as well as the drive to acquire material goods at any cost, have superseded the desire for godliness and right living to the place where worldly possessions now take precedence. In addition, social demons like crime, sex, drugs and alcohol have become alternative solutions that seduce the souls and minds of Blacks. Unfortunately, pleasure and things have captured Blacks as they have other races. Sexual freedom and self-expression have climbed to the top of the charts in importance.

The root cause is a lack of a clear and positive cultural identity. As a race, the black people have overcome many roadblocks along the way. But perhaps the greatest one has yet to be defeated--a lack of appreciation for the strong Christian foundation necessary to clearly evaluate ourselves. This struggle to be affirmed by the world's system has skewed our perception of what is valuable. As a result, many have gone down the wrong road, making politically correct decisions at the expense of morally incorrect choices.

In a quest to attain fame and fortune, the moral fiber and integrity of the Black race has come under severe attack. The tragedy is that this same identity demon is silently decaying the morals of those in the middle and upper classes. These mistakenly believe that they have arrived and ignore all the signs, including high divorce rates, crime statistics, drug and alcohol dependence and deteriorating moral values. Just because we refuse to come to terms with the problems facing Black America doesn't mean they will go away. Only God can solve what ails our culture. Blacks must recognize that they have a significant moral and spiritual crisis facing them, and move to seek God's love, confirmation and restoration. Blacks can overcome the deterioration within their families and race by aborting the pursuit of selfish pleasure that ultimately leads to self-destruction.

The black church must commit to helping its people with the larger self-esteem issue. The answer will not be found in bigger and more prestigious church buildings, but rather in a moral and upright people walking together in love and truth. A holistic approach is necessary to counteract the hidden struggle Blacks face with self-worth.

In the beginning God created man, including Blacks, with a healthy self-image. Slavery helped to destroy that image. In contemporary Black America, the moral direction of the majority greatly impacts the culture at large. The negative effects of slavery and self-inflicted wounds can be reversed through relationship and fellowship with Jesus Christ. It is only through relationship with God that we can achieve a sense of belonging and positive identity.

TWO

Evidence of a Problem

The evening news begins with another drive-by-shooting that has just claimed the life of another black teenage male. These types of incidents are routine so why be alarmed? Today, a two-year old child died from a bullet that had no name on it. Though it was meant for someone else, that child was in the wrong place at the wrong time. The newscaster follows with several other accounts of violence in the suburbs and the city. Then the news follows with the reporting of a domestic disturbance that ends with a man murdering his estranged wife, before finally turning the gun on himself.

The world news related similar accounts, including the genocide of its own people by an African nation. The newspapers report these stories day after day, and customers buy newspapers, watch news reports and proceed about business as usual. But life is forever changed in households that have lost loved ones. And some never recover from that loss.

Over the years, many of these stories have been aired on the evening news. But what happens to those whose loved ones were killed? In metropolitan areas across the country the stories are the same. At one time it was thought that these stories only occurred in the inner cities. Today, we know better, because murders and violent crimes are also increasing in the suburbs. We can no longer escape to the suburbs believing we are safe from harm. It seems that we are a nation at war both overseas and at home. While terrorists have created fear in our nation, there is another fear that looms large every day. We have become a nation where hearing that someone has been murdered does not disturb us much, unless it is one of our own. Why is there so much tragedy and violence in a country where **"In God we trust" is inscribed on its money?** The love of this same money has perpetuated much of the black crime problem. Drugs and money laundering flourish day after day. Not only that, but another victim will fall from the bullet of someone who values money more than life.

Statistics support the fact that Blacks commit most violent crimes. Is this true or not? Are Blacks more violent than other nationalities? There is some evidence that would tend to suggest that. I am not here to argue the statistics but to raise the question, "Does anyone care about the mistaken value we place on material things?" Our playgrounds have become battlegrounds. In many respects, we are a nation at war with itself. Less than seventy-five years ago, the current level of violence was unheard of. In a sense, we have forgotten those things that should matter most, and gone a-whoring after other things. What has happened to the Black race that has caused it to become so angry and to forget to "love thy neighbor as thyself"? Both the government and the church have tried to weigh in on the problem but have had little success. Have black people become a people with a stolen identity? What about Dr. Martin Luther King's dream--have we forgotten it? Where is God in the Black race's search for their lost identity? Can He show them how to find it again?

Some 400 years ago Blacks came to this country as a non-violent people. They were not a hostile race, and in fact became enslaved without resistance. So, what happened that led to this change? I'm not certain we'd find the answer even after examining all the possibilities, but one thing is certain:

prisons are overcrowded with black males, and Black families are too often left fatherless.

Just yesterday evening a news story aired about a shooting in the nation's capital where another black male died and another is now behind bars awaiting trial. And today, more than likely another incident will take place. In fact, this past week has been fraught with violence. Four Amish children died at the hands of a man who planned to harm someone else. This proves that violence is not always committed by a single race of people. But knowing this does nothing to solve the escalating violence within the black community and within our nation as a whole. Numerous criminology books have been released that deal with crime and the black community. Many Blacks live in comfortable and even luxurious homes. So, what is the problem with our people? Clearly, it takes more than nice things to obtain a healthy identity.

During my college years, there was great pride in being Black. In fact, I recall various events and occasions where blackness was highlighted and Blacks boasted about their blackness with pride. At the Junior College I attended, there were several groups who considered blackness as something that would lead to trouble, yet blacks continued to look at their race with pride and dignity. There was no high crime rate on campus or in the inner city where the college was located. Fighting was done not with weapons but with fists, because there was a sense of pride in not destroying one's brother or sister. The worst crimes involved theft but usually ended without violence, and men did not walk down the street packing a gun. Back then, life was much more safe and pleasant. People attended social gatherings without shooting each other. Husbands and wives managed their domestic problems with much less violence. And if we tracked the increase of violence over the last ten to fifteen years, we would have to agree that something has changed. Blacks have gone from being a passive people to becoming easily angered and bent toward violence.

Two days ago I was sharing with someone my concern about the level of violence in our nation. I mentioned how our ancestors struggled against the evil system of slavery and how we are now ushering in our own system of slavery. We must begin to take a hard look at what headlines fill the news and newspapers each day. Then, we must look at how much economic progress we've made only to be dampened by the lack of spiritual and moral love for each other. A well-known comedian recently spoke of how the Black's world has drastically changed. Afterward other Blacks grew angry with him for speaking about a problem we can no longer ignore. I agree wholeheartedly with that comedian, except I feel even more strongly about our situation and why we must change to help save our heritage. If we continue in the direction we are going, what will the history books say about the Black race? That long and hard-won legacy of Black accomplishments against slavery could be forever marred because we've lost our identity. To understand the identity struggle of the black people we must first examine those pivotal moments in our nation's past.

THREE

The Black Journey

Several centuries ago a black people were brought to America for the purpose of slavery. Slavery will forever impact the issues facing all of us in contemporary America. Perhaps there will never be a true measure of the overall damage caused by slavery, but we can all agree that it did harm our culture.

The black race is distinctive in many ways. Its language differs vastly from that of other cultures. Slaves brought with them a vast amount of knowledge and a distinctive way of communicating. The black culture's food choices and methods of preparation were also different from those of other cultures. Their clothing and customs were different. Although they were taken out of their native land by force, they held onto much of their heritage and beliefs. It was these distinctive differences between the blacks and white America that became the "Black identity experience."

What did the term originally mean? To many of the people who had never been enslaved the phrase was little more than a passing fad. But to those who had it meant something more. It became a collection of customs, doctrines, emotions, feelings and beliefs that united them as a people. Most of the themes that currently characterize the black experience are rooted in early black tradition. Terms like *soul, brother* and *sister* all existed within ordinary folk culture, first on the plantation and later the ghetto. Other elements became celebrated as part of early folk culture. Long ago William E.B. Dubois developed the simple but powerful motto, "Black is beautiful." Others argued for education that included sociological studies and a collective appreciation of the black culture. Other features of the black experience became themes of literature, jazz, religion and other spiritual endeavors.

The reader may ask the question, "What does this phrase "Black is Beautiful" have to do with being black today?" It's hard to find a phrase that fits today, and if there is one, it's probably not one we would be proud to own, because it describes an often desperate experience.

Such a phrase may seem inconceivable in the minds of non-blacks, because until the early sixties, the term had not been defined, but once it was, everything began to change.

Because it was an insult to be called "black" at that time, they called themselves "colored." It wasn't long before people who once tried to escape the slave identity began to seek self-fulfillment. After a time they found themselves thinking of their color and heritage as beautiful.

The surprising thing about this blackness phenomenon is that it made such a sudden and deep impact on black young people. It was as life-changing as an old-fashioned spiritual revival or an African ritual ceremony that suddenly captured the attention of everyone, whether black or white. The "Black is beautiful" era was, for the very first time, characterized by a state of euphoria or pleasant feelings about being Black. I have to wonder why it took nearly 400 years before this tiny, three-word phrase would make the world recognize us as a distinct but valuable culture. Could it be that Blacks in slavery were content to be called colored or "nigger"? If so, then it is conceivable that Blacks in the sixties saw a need to be identified as something more and demanded a status change.

On the other hand, could it be that Blacks, who had never seen themselves this way before, were suddenly "aware" of their own value? Whatever the reason, it brought about a sudden and revolutionary change in identity. For the first time, Blacks had a new and deeper appreciation of what it meant to be black, but because they failed to grasp the need for cultural responsibility and accountability, they would later lose this new black awareness. This failure was complete, encompassing spiritual, philosophical and moral aspects of life.

So who was responsible for this new awareness? Clearly God in his wisdom saw a need to deliver a people out of an "Egypt situation." Stimulated by racial problems and the ideas of a new breed of leaders, including Malcolm X, Stokley Carmichael, and Rap Brown, themes that had lain dormant in the black culture were suddenly making headlines. Regardless of who is responsible, blackness emerged as both cause and consequence of racial conflict. Through the crucible of conflict, black youths came to see themselves as active, assertive, and self-actualized. A new sense of self-worth emerged as a result of these experiences.

Eager to identify with blackness, young Blacks now saw themselves with new freedom, displaying both independence and pride that soon became associated with that expression, "I am Black and I'm proud." At that point, this new sense of pride was expressed in the dress and grooming of black people. These distinctions became even more visible in Afro grooming, distinctive clothing, and different foods that became collectively known as soul food.

The new black experience also led to racial conflict in the riots of the late sixties. Racial conflict was in essence a struggle for significance. This new sense of self-worth and pride led to a problem for America. For the first time in history Blacks felt a sense of accomplishment and sought for more of this thing called freedom. But what difference did it make for young Blacks to wear Afro hairstyles or wear different clothes or eat different food? From the Blacks' perspective, it meant they had something to call their own that would preserve their ancestral heritage. To a black child, it meant that he did not have to pursue straight hair and white skin, but could admire the darkness of his skin, and curly hair.

Further, he was enabled to feel proud to seek out activities inside his own race, where he could explore and define his likes and dislikes. I can identify with this discovery because of my own past experiences. Being an individual creates a sense of self-respect and pride for which every person yearns. But there is more to this experience than feeling excited about it or being told that it was available. It opened for Blacks a new world of dreams apart from the old institution of slavery, a history they desperately wanted to forget. The slavery era became known as the "mark of oppression," and damage could be traced within the American racial struggle over the centuries. In modern times the term initially became associated with the dual problems of segregation and discrimination.

The years just after the end of slavery found the Black race yearning for its own identity. At least a portion of today's problems can be traced back to that era.

Enslavement had left a deep and ugly scar. The "mark of oppression" forced the Black race to rise up and identify with its African culture. While black awareness was not the complete answer for a race with no cultural identity in America at that time, it did help push an end to the slavery mentality. It was a partial answer because it gave Blacks one mark of distinction apart from their past oppressor, white society. Individual Blacks moved from just wanting to be seen as persons of value to actually needing a culture with which to identify, which occurred in the "Black experience."

What was the black experience? What did it have to do with the search of a people for its identity? I would define it this way: the search for identity apart from a negative slave past. It is that psychological awareness where blacks see themselves invited to act like others, different from themselves in the social arena. Further, it may be defined as a time when blacks discovered the birth of joy, progress and achievement in simply being black. They learned that this state of being would have a direct bearing on the rest of their lives. They would always be able to trace their history and think of the degradation their ancestors endured. By the mercies of God, a people once in slavery, was now free. Degradation and heartache ultimately led to new opportunities and positive change.

Within the black community, the black experience helped the Black race to move into the future with some degree of optimism. To many, the black experience meant knowing that though you may not have been accepted as fully human, you were thankful to no longer be enslaved. Others may have wondered what life would have been like had they not felt the pain of discrimination in one form or another. The black experience often meant a daily grind with no dream and no possibility of a dream, to illuminate a sad and lonely journey.

It felt much like suffering through mental abuse and oppression and then escaping the chains that bound us. Someone might describe it as the "collective experience of a people living within a population, but largely outside of American civilization." Regardless of how you view the black experience, it had an impact on those who lived it.

Along with the black experience came the terms "soul" and "Blacks." This soul had nothing to do with the Bible or the soul of man. It involved Blacks expressing themselves within the American culture, searching for independence and identity. This constant search for cultural identity enabled them to stumble upon another admirable distinction--the search for soul gave additional purpose to a people with no identity. To have soul meant you could be yourself, and didn't have to be anyone else. To early Blacks it meant being born again into their own heritage. It became something to hold onto that could not be taken away. Blacks had discovered a new beauty in being black. To talk about Black soul spoke of awaking from a period of shame to express one's belief in one's true beauty and learning to appreciate the black skin that was once such a disappointment.

The term "soul" referred to that period when Blacks felt thrilled to be true to themselves, authentic regarding their feelings and emotions. Soul can be expressed in many arenas, including music, art, food, clothing and talk distinctly different from those of mainstream America. Blacks had finally created a separate identity to claim as their own, a unique identity that applied only to them, excluding all other races. I read a book that said the term "soul" involved three components: spontaneity, feelings, and spirituality.

As a result of this new thought process, blackness was now transformed into a positive thing in the mind of Blacks. They could say "Look, I am black and beautiful because I have been blessed with soul."

During this period, the term "soul food" also became popular in the black culture. Soul food included a quickly evolving collection of recipes and dishes that were available during the lean days of the Civil War and Reconstruction. These dishes included parts left after the butchering of swine, as well as greens, sweet potatoes, peas, beans and the like. These foods were prepared with certain seasonings that distinguished them as being unique to the Blacks, another way to break away from the white culture and distinguish them as separate and distinct. The black awareness experience made soul food a source of pride among Black people.

"Soul talk" became a common but distinctive type of speech, a simple, "jive," trash talking, a mode of kidding and flattery among Blacks in social conversation. There were several styles of soul talk dispersed within the black culture. These included the Barber shop informal gathering, sports activities talk, and the more serious church and work conversations. Soul talk was a unique system of communication of gestures and spontaneity within the intimate, inclusive world of Blacks. So what did all this soul talk mean to the Black man? It gave him his own system of communication. With this unique language system, he was able to feel comfortable without being intimidated into having to use another culture's language patterns. Obviously, when conversing with other races, he would have to use their language. But when communicating only in the Black community, he felt free to use this soul talk. Having their own language made Blacks feel proud, even though it was slang talk, because it meant they had mastered a second language. To many blacks, being bilingual was a source of great dignity and pride, especially after being forced to adapt to the language of others for so long.

In our contemporary world Blacks still use much of that slang language to communicate with each other. A good example is "Blood, you and I are grooving together." Both Blacks and other cultures are familiar with such talk.

Romantic conversations often contain slang expressions. For example, most of the black lyrics and blues recordings of yesterday and today had their roots in those early slang expressions. These were said to have stirred the Blacks' emotions after a hard day at work. They tapped each person's spirit, feelings and spontaneity. While soul talk had its place in the struggle of the Black people, it must never become misconstrued to mean the 'soul' that God has given to every human.

Black music was another phenomenon that had an early impact on Blacks and their struggle for an identity. The music of Blacks is an authentic expression of the black mystique and includes: jazz, spirituals, blues, and gospels. Songs in these modes were often traditional, emerging from the dim and unknown slave past, and later composed for the commercial music market. These traditions are both sacred and secular, but those distinctions were not always clear. A soulful lament can refer to either a love relationship or the suffering for Jesus. Only the words distinguished many of the various black musical pieces. Unless outsiders were familiar with Black music, they might not understand its original meaning. Black music, both during and after slavery, had a certain kind of rhythm to it. Intentionally composed, it is distinctive to its own culture, allowing Blacks to claim it as their own invention.

Through their music the slaves were able to communicate their emotions and heartache. The long days in the fields were spent chanting hymns and other traditional native songs peculiar to the slaves and their ancestors. To other races, it made little sense. It was this music that strengthened them to endure hard life on the plantation, allowing them to identify with each other and their own culture. Their music marked the discovery of one more cultural feature that was natural, beautiful and distinct and for some, brought great rewards, even fame and fortune. A partial list of performers includes: Aretha Franklin, Mahalia Jackson, James Brown, Rev. Shirley Caesar, Kirk Franklin, and the Hawkins family.

Black composers and poets also emerged from that post-slavery era. Many Black composers and songwriters have become famous for their musical talent.

Stage plays are another means that black society used to convey their soulful cultural messages, displaying their gifts and talents, as well as their natural creativity.

FOUR

Blacks and Politics

What was it like being Black within the political structure of early America? At that time, a black man was completely excluded from top posts in the political arena. Because he was excluded from the political decision-making process, he learned to accept his limitations and cultivated other ways to employ his new awareness. Simply, he learned to accept the fact that he would never be a dominant political leader. He learned to operate within the system in the only way he could.

During the slavery era, the black population had no vote or voice. In fact, subsequent to the slave era, Blacks were kept away from the polls by the Ku Klux Klan and other groups who wanted to prevent Blacks from having a voice. Federal laws were passed that finally gave Blacks the privilege to express themselves at the polls. They saw this as another door of opportunity to move further from the "mark of oppression" that had so defined them. For the first time in history, Blacks had unlimited freedom within the political arena. However, the passage of these laws did not stop illegal voting practices. Even though Blacks were now legally able to vote, there were Whites who had no intention of letting that happen. In fact, in many cases Blacks were considered only one-fifth human. And even when they could, many Blacks never voiced their opinions and preferences through the polls. Voting laws did not stop Blacks from being assaulted or even killed trying to exercise that new found right to vote. In other cases, employers would deny Blacks the opportunity to get off from work to vote. Many were intimidated with threats of firing if they chose to leave without their employers' permission. And though political free expression was for a long time a difficult struggle, they refused to be denied the right to vote. Sadly, freedom from the plantation did not necessarily grant Blacks the right to express themselves politically nor socially. At that time, race relegated Blacks to a lower class.

The Blacks concentrated in central ghettos were alienated from both major political parties. However, that alienation seemed to be a pre-cursor toward political freedom. In the ghettos, the black population found themselves facing a future of self-realization and self-assurance. Along with this new level of confidence, they felt a new kind of pride and self-worth after the success of Black economic boycotts, housing possessions, and voting rights initiatives. With this new feeling of self-assurance black leaders began to enter the political arena as mayors and city councilmen, but they had yet to be elected to major political positions. Blacks realized that had it not been for certain powerful white brothers and sisters, their political success would have taken twice as long. There were key White political figures who pushed for the rights of Negros, as the black people were then called. Together, they broke the barrier, paving the way for those who were formerly slaves, to achieve political status and power. By 1970, four cities with black ghettos had finally achieved a long sought-after accomplishment, representation by Blacks in politics. Political expression was a new victory for the entire black population. Through that new voice other social changes were now possible.

In the early period following their success in the political arena, they found themselves not decision makers but pawns in a huge political machine. They were not given major roles in leadership. Their political hope was one of chance, controlled, or at least dictated by others, and this led to a feeling of political apathy. Although they had the privilege to vote, they saw themselves with no power to change their circumstances.

One of the bright spots for Blacks in politics was the steady growth and influence of a liberal White element. The opportunity to vote in southern states was a step in the right direction for Blacks. For the first time many states promised to appoint Blacks to positions they had never held before. For example, black candidates were now appointed to city council and police forces. Never had a black policeman been appointed in a southern state until political pressure was applied.

In the majority of the southern states voting remained risky business for most black people. Intimidation and violence were still used to prevent the black voter from free expression at the polls. This was the only way to keep Blacks in an inferior position within the establishment. They knew that if Blacks were free to vote, the old system of white supremacy would die, and because the social arena would soon undergo massive change, the distribution of political power would also change.

Through most of this era, Blacks played an insignificant role. Most Blacks were limited to inferior tasks such as carrying messages and serving on support committees. Although they lent their support to those in positions of power, Blacks were overlooked when assignments were made. Other black elected persons were paid off with menial jobs in the city halls and courthouses. Only a few were lucky enough to get jobs that made a difference. And if they did, they were only put in as standbys.

Such positions included: ministers, teachers, policemen and others elected to keep the status quo order of the day. They were employed to allay confusion as interpreters to the at-large political action groups. They spoke to White decision makers and passed down those decisions to the black population. These representatives were used to control tension, facilitate communication, and keep black order. The line of communication, however, flowed only one way, from the top to those at the bottom, the Blacks.

A black representative could talk to the leaders but he had no influence nor did he have any say once a decision was made. In all truth, these representatives were used to separate the leaders from the rank-and-file members. This system of political communication was organized so that white political leaders could give the impression of sharing political power and wealth, when in reality they were there to serve in the role of scapegoat. In this way, White leaders could avoid having to deal with the black rank-and-file members. This scenario never produced any real changes for the Blacks. It was just the way things were, and everyone accepted it.

The politics of nonviolence in the South found some success under Dr. Martin Luther King during the 1960s. Dr. King took his struggle to the northern cities, while Rev. Jesse Jackson launched a boycotting movement called Operation Breadbasket that instituted a change from the philosophy of Dr. King. Dr. King ushered in social and political changes to both the South and the North. But perhaps the greatest change was in shaking of the foundation of America, forcing it to recognize that it had not lived up to its democratic principles. Now its democratic principles went through a period of testing, not simply in theory, but in practice.

In spite of the achievements of the mass nonviolence movement, many northern states were not really changed by the movement, and success was not as widespread as many had been led to believe. Most of the political challenge to democracy concentrated on bringing changes to the South. In the meantime, the North was not under such scrutiny nor was it evaluated on its own merit. Political changes were needed to redirect the course of America once and for all.

The term, "political riots' is not simply a metaphor for civil unrest, but describes a real series of events that would forever change the American culture. It is essential that we understand how these race riots influenced the growth of political liberty for black people. Riots came about because of a failure of society to change a repressed system and recognize minorities. Though Dr. King limited his movement to nonviolence there was early evidence that the movement would be short-lived; clearly his movement would be under pressure from both black militants and White society. It would have limited results that would eventually antagonize his own people. Black militants were waiting, eager to see Dr. King's movement fail. They were impatient with his methods and wanted to use more violent means to initiate change. It was only a matter of time before violence would erupt.

The government's lack of response to Dr. King's demands for change played into the hands of militant blacks. On one hand America had a repressed system, and on the other an impatient black population that had waited too long for equality. Why did America refuse to alter its political system? Many historians today wonder why things were not done to prevent a revolution. Perhaps White America believed that Blacks would never challenge the system in such a violent manner. They neglected to look at history, where at one time or another, oppressed people have rebelled against the systems that oppressed them. In this case, Blacks took America by surprise and lashed out with violence. Many will argue that this was unnecessary, that social changes would have occurred eventually anyway.

What were some of the changes? For the first time in history, black people recognized the enormity of the power they possessed. They actually saw their power in action, watching as the social structure was shaken and the Whites rushed to stabilize it. They also realized they did not have to remain an oppressed race. Dr. King already knew this when he challenged America to morally evaluate itself.

Two other offshoots of the riots were the birth of Black Nationalism and politics of the revolution. Both movements used power to influence society outside of the white establishment. Black nationalists sought to manipulate the political system, whereas Black revolutionists wanted to tear down and reconstruct the entire social system, completely reversing the power structure. This, of course, never materialized. Dr. King was not interested in further corrupting the social order, but rather required it to correct what was wrong and share the power with the black population. While riots contributed to the success of Blacks in the political arena, the affects of such means left a permanent scar on America.

What is political success, and why was it so important that Blacks help to shape their future? To the black population as a whole, it marked an era when everyone could participate equally in the political process without regard to skin color. While this was a dream for Blacks, it was somewhat unrealistic, because at that time, such a dream was not even a reality for all Whites.

The sixties and seventies saw many positive political changes including the election of Blacks in all parts of the country. During this period, there was a tremendous increase in blacks in state legislatures, city councils and among county commissioners.

What caused this second revolution in politics? A primary reason was the social structure of the cities. During the early years city ghettos came about and the white residents moved to the suburbs. The Blacks not only inherited the cities the whites had left behind but also all the problems. Once again, they were forced to band together to solve the many problems confronting black people. With no other logical options, black leaders immediately joined forces to resolve these issues. The leaders and the community as a whole became more cohesive, self-conscious and confident. It was the desertion of the cities by white residents that eventually ushered in a new day for Blacks. This change in the social system would give birth to a new black recognition.

At last, the white political superiority was giving away some of it political power to the black people. Unfortunately Blacks made many mistakes in governing the inner cities but learned important lessons from their errors. Eventually black leaders corrected those errors, becoming more confident of their political ability, and went on to contribute to the black political process.

A new philosophy grew out of this new black confidence. Black leaders continued to lash out at an institutional order to establish justice for all. New and peaceful efforts were implemented to obtain democracy for everyone, after Blacks realized that changes gained through nonviolence were the only lasting political changes. Thus nonviolence became the means to implementing lasting changes. Only when all races cooperated to seek lasting political freedom for everyone did real political maturity begin to take place.

The implication that political changes have had for Blacks since slavery can be summed up in the simple phrase, "to achieve political balance." The future of black people and the political process must be based upon a desire to see justice for all, and not just for Blacks. Those black ancestors had patience and understood that while freedom is not easily achieved, it offers benefits to those willing to pursue rights God intended for everyone.

Can a balance be achieved by achieving an equal ratio of black people in political office? I don't know, and I'm not sure that this is necessary to accomplish political balance. The key word for black people is "time." It was years before a black city councilman was elected, but it finally did happen. I believe that absolute political justice is unrealistic in some sense. Blacks must focus upon making political progress through responsible efforts. These efforts cannot be maintained except through following spiritual principles and assuming moral obligations. The question we must ask is "Have we failed to appreciate the struggles of those ancestors who died for political justice?" Many years have come and gone since the first black person was allowed to vote. We must understand the high cost they paid for the privilege we have today.

A strong respect for the blackness experience opened the once denied opportunity for Blacks. For once, Blacks could awaken and take another look at themselves. Up until the black awareness movement, Blacks found nothing unique to them. It encouraged the black population to search for some feature that could force the American society to take a second look and acknowledge their distinctly black cultural assets. Prior to the black awareness revolution, they were a race of people with little to cheer about. So, to those Blacks who knew the plight of their ancestors, the awareness revolution was a blessing from God. It gave them dignity and a reason to keep pushing for political and social changes.

Perhaps the upcoming presidential election will reveal a lot about the political maturity of Blacks. The candidates include a woman and a black man. The nomination of either will depend largely upon the vote of the Black population.

FIVE

Cultural Contributions of Blacks

More than 350 years ago Blacks began making meaningful contributions to this nation. Cultural contributions are unique and meaningful, bringing a feeling of pride to every race of people, and Blacks are no exception. It is this pride that instills confidence that their race did not just come and go, leaving behind no valuable heritage.

The first black settlers were patriots, men and women of character, and younger blacks should view them as role models to emulate. They paved the way to make life better for all mankind.

Black contributions can be traced from the beginning of their arrival around 1620. Though enslaved, they bought with them a vast amount of knowledge and wisdom to share with their masters. Their skills and physical prowess made them valuable to those they served, and increased the demand for their service, beginning during the Pilgrim era. Black servants showed wisdom and intelligence and had developed practical cooking skills as well as an incredible grasp of survival skills that proved essential to their masters during hard times. They patiently served others without becoming rebellious. It took courage, strength and self-discipline to serve with the right attitude.

It would take many volumes to trace the cultural contributions of a proud black race to this nation. Most would agree that had it not been for the developments and inventions of the black people, America would not be the nation it is today. One cannot help but notice the beauty and simplicity of the black influence throughout our environment.

After their arrival on American shores, their physical strength would become the backbone of America's agricultural industry. The enslavement of those black ancestors was a choice among several alternatives available to the colonists to increase the economic value of the plantation.

That choice meant that Europeans would abandon the principle of democracy and create an organized system of forced labor. Because the early American system was governed by a mercantile economy and the philosophical ideology to support a slave mentality, Blacks became a dream come true for white plantation owners. Codifying the principles of slavery created a deep insecurity in the black American slave, along with the destruction of his dignity, and the elimination of the sanctity of his family. A single drop of black blood could condemn one to a slave status.

The owner had every right to the black slave as well as his labor and services. Before long, the institution of slavery had become a sophisticated mechanism for developing the model slave. The slave was kept constantly disciplined; implanted in his mind was a belief in his inferiority; the enormity of his master's power was held over him at all times. Before long, he had developed a child-like dependence upon his master and all members of the ruling class.

The philosophy that America used to justify their independence from Great Britain stimulated the black people to initiate petitions for their own freedom. At that time certain revolutionary colonists recognized their inconsistency as oppressors and slaveholders, and decided to do something about it. Men like Benjamin Franklin and

Benjamin Rush were among the first to call for action. Blacks will always be indebted to those leaders who began the abolition movement. But credit must also be given to those compassionate white leaders who led the fight for black freedom. We must credit those liberal Whites and black slave leaders who delivered the final death knell to the institution of slavery.

If Blacks had not begun that long struggle to organize and walk out of bondage, slavery would have survived even longer. But once Blacks began to organize, the power structure of white America dwindled and some of the organizational skills were shared with black leaders who then became spokesmen for Blacks both during and after slavery. And while history proves that excellent leadership was the key that determined the success of the abolition movement, we owe gratitude to God and his vision to lead Blacks out of their Egypt. God used those white leaders to be as angels of light to lead dark souls out of hell. Blacks must never forget their contribution toward the freedom of the black race.

A serious campaign for the freedom of black people was started by slaves in Boston around 1770. Several black slaves joined forces to petition the assembly for their emancipation so that they could be transported to some part of the coast of their native Africa to settle. Among these courageous souls were Sambo Freeman, Chester Joie, and Peter Bestes. Other groups later challenged the courts on the constitutionality of white supremacy to own slaves. The courts heard case after case, demanding to know how a nation that fled from the religious enslavement in England now pursued a system it had earlier condemned. Black leaders continued to search for legal mechanisms that could assist them in proving that slavery was irrational and unconstitutional. Other indentured slaves sued their owners for promising freedom that never came. Jane Drew and John Siffin led the way in using the courts to sue their owners. Although they won their cases, the legal system was too slow and expensive to constitute a major force toward their emancipation. But both the petitions and the lawsuits served to foster anti-slavery activities that eventually brought about emancipation.

Black leadership did not stop fighting because the system failed to address their rights. In fact, Blacks even served and died fighting for their country. Crispus Attucks, a black man from Boston, became the first American to die for independence during the Boston Massacre. Blacks followed Attucks into combat reinforcing the slaves' demand for a role in the Revolutionary War. Despite many obstacles, Blacks were persistent in their efforts to contribute to America as part of the armed forces. There were also black soldiers who served with General George Washington.

The black leaders who died in the armed forces did not die in vain. Their contributions to this nation and the Black race will never be forgotten. Subsequent to the end of slavery in the north, Blacks began to make progress in their struggle to be free. Despite obstacles the black leadership remained determined to lead their people to freedom. During this time, Blacks made incredible contributions. Some of these include: Phyllis Wheatley, who was an admired colonial poet. Benjamin Banneker, another slave made great discoveries in the field of astronomy, and was appointed to assist in the survey of Washington, DC. Paul Cuffe became an early leader in the shipbuilding industry. John Chavis, a minister of the Presbyterian Church developed private schools, where he educated some of the outstanding leaders in the South.

There were many black leaders who spearheaded the abolitionist movement. Several forces contributed to their effectiveness: growing anti-slavery writings, great strides in education of a free black people, and the political conflicts surrounding the legality of slave ownership. Despite the laws of the southern states that restricted the education of slaves, many black leaders led the way in speaking out against the inhumane institution of slavery. Nat Turner and David Walker led the way, inciting slaves to rebel against their owners. Nat Turner became one of the first to help black people escape north to freedom, by sponsoring an underground railroad effort. Perhaps the greatest contributors toward the abolitionist movement were ex-slaves in the northern states who sponsored efforts to free southern slaves. Fredrick Douglas was one of the most instrumental and eloquent leaders responsible for the success of the abolition movement. He published newspapers that advocated the Blacks' right to be free.

Few would dare argue against the vital role Nat Turner played during this era, encouraging slaves to revolt. Turner and others continued to push slave-owning states toward abolition. He was later captured and hanged for the murder of his owner and others, but he did not give his life in vain, for although it did not come until many years after Turner's death, slavery was finally abolished.

Another outstanding abolitionist was Harriet Tubman, who became one, if not *the* greatest leader in the underground movement. She is credited for leading over 300 slaves to freedom. During the war she served as a nurse and a spy for General Grant. I would daresay that if you mention the word *slavery* or the phrase *abolition movement* Harriet Tubman's name would come to mind.

Among others revered for their contributions to freeing the slaves, the names of William Trotter, William Dubois and Marcus Garvey are well-known for their devotion, intelligence and courage during this era. Although we might disapprove of their militant methods, we must respect their efforts to abolish slavery. These leaders envisioned God's destiny for Blacks to be free. Trotter was imprisoned for his militant efforts, and Dubois and others carried on the fight, becoming a leader in the NAACP. (National Association for the Advancement of Colored People) Marcus Garvey was the last radical militant who advocated that black people should leave America and return to Africa. He pushed for colonization of Africa because he felt that there would be no justice for black people in America. His movement failed, never getting off the ground.

Two key organizations during that time included: CORE (Congress of Racial Equality), and the NAACP. They pushed for equal rights for black people through positive, nonviolent means. These groups were an offshoot of the Ghanaian movement. This technique became known as nonviolent direct action and used boycotts and other nonviolent methods to bring about change. The NAACP was organized by Whites to bring about economic, political, and social changes that would benefit Blacks. It was more successful than any other organization at influencing court decisions regarding Black civil liberties. The goal of these organizations was to promote black recognition in a country where it had previously been denied.

Whenever we think of black leadership, there is no one who deserves more recognition than Dr. Martin Luther King Jr. He probably never reached his zenith of influence due to his tragic early death. He believed that all people were created by God to be free and have an equal opportunity for a descent life. His ideas were pure and spiritually free of prejudice. Perhaps this is what I admired most about Dr. King: his effort to bring about change was not just for Blacks but for all people through nonviolent means. Although many of his followers reverted to other more violent means to implement change, Dr. King refused to stoop to violence as a means to a spiritual end. Through his devotion, both Blacks and Whites saw God's plan carried out in love. His results gave black people some hope in a white-dominated world. His determination to use biblical principles to accomplish God's vision distinguished his legacy from those of others of his day. Love rather than hate marked the work of Dr. King.

Blacks also made immense contributions to America's scientific discoveries and inventions. Many of these contributions were never recorded or were credited to other nationalities. Only recently were many of these outstanding black leaders recognized for their cultural gifts. Some have never before been acknowledged.

George Washington Carver was one of the greatest scientists in United States history. He became famous for discovering the many uses for the peanut, which was used in the manufacture of over 100 products.

Within his brief life span, Dr. Charles Drew made incredible contributions to medicine. After graduating from Howard University, he went on to become a pathologist in our nation's capital, as well as one of the nation's greatest scientists. His research in the field of transfusions and blood-typing became the new standard for the medical procedures during his day. When you mention medical advances, Drew's name tops the list.

Blacks also made great strides as explorers and adventurers. James Beckwourth and Jean Baptiste were the black Lewis and Clark of their day, exploring much of the undiscovered wilderness and mountainous areas that have become the inhabited parklands of our day.

In the field of drama and literary work, names like Sidney Poitier, Langston Hughes, and Ralph Emerson quickly come to mind. At one time Blacks were not allowed major roles in the theatre, and in fact, it took 150 years for this breakthrough to occur, but eventually it did. Paul Robeson and Poitier will always be remembered for their sincere and distinctive acting ability. Robeson was known as one of the great actors and singers of his time. Not only did he become famous in America but internationally as well.

Redd Foxx, Bill Cosby, Moms Mabley, Richard Pryor excelled in the field of television comedy. While the humor of some of these comedians was sometimes sexually explicit, they combined humor with wit to entertain the world and warm the hearts of those around them. They were able to break into a white-dominated world and leave a mark that not only pleased the black people but people of all races.

Other Blacks who made tremendous literary and dramatic contributions include: Phyllis Wheatley, Sojourner Truth, Billy Dee Williams, and Rosa Parks. Parks' refusal to give up her seat to a White person led to the first anti-segregation strike, which took place in Montgomery, Alabama. Sojourner Truth was a talented author and Black crusader. Since slavery, Black writers have excelled not only in poetry but in short stories, novels, and textbooks. For a long time black slaves were forbidden to read and write, though some learned in spite of the rules. From those early days came writers who had an uncanny talent for poetry. No one knows exactly how and why black people excelled in the literary arts, but they did. It is my personal belief that their slavery environment actually contributed to their ability to talk and later write about their experiences. Having lived through the dread and abuse of the slave era, those black ancestors passionately described their pain as no one else could. These people had a story to tell and recorded their inner feelings on parchment for future generations to appreciate.

Then there was Langston Hughes, a genius in the literary world; no one was greater as a poet and writer. He wrote about political life in America and its impact upon black people. More than any other figure, Hughes gave black people a sense of hope for the future. American youth can learn much from the work ethics of those early black leaders, who, like Hughes, advocated hard work and long hours to succeed. Their success came about because of setting a goal and striving diligently to make it happen.

Blacks have also made outstanding contributions in the field of sports. While some of these had natural talent, others had to work hard to become recognized as leaders in their field. Hank Aaron, Willie Mays, Joe Louis, Muhammad Ali, Jackie Robinson, Wilt Chamberlain, Bill Russell, Shaquille O'Neal, Tiger Woods, the Williams sisters, O. J. Simpson, and Jim Brown are but a few of the leaders in the sports field. Blacks can be proud of their unusual athletic talent. In fact, athletic ability has been a way out of the ghetto projects for many Blacks who went on to become role models in culturally-deprived neighborhoods, their contributions recorded in history books. These leaders proved that anyone could become successful if he was willing to devote the time and effort to master necessary skills.

Black contributions to the music industry, especially vocal music were legendary. In fact the cotton fields and plantation kitchens became stages as they sang to help them endure life as slaves. They learned to sing hymns and spirituals to cope with their hurt and degradation. Modern day leaders in the field include: Mahalia Jackson, Stevie Wonder, Aretha Franklin, Rev. Shirley Caesar, Marvin Gaye, James Brown, the father of soul; Dianna Ross, Michael Jackson, Kirk Franklin, Rev. James Cleveland, to name but a few.

It has been my hope to stimulate remembrance of those Blacks who made significant contributions to society. Although most of our society is aware of the athletic contributions of Blacks, most do not know much about Blacks' scientific and literary accomplishments. In the entertainment industry, we're probably more familiar with modern day rappers and hip-hop singers than those of the past. Only recently has more emphasis been placed on recording and remembering those early black slaves and their great contributions to the world. Even today, much of the historical information about slave life and the struggles for freedom have gone unrecorded.

All races must educate themselves so that their struggles for freedom will not go on unnoticed. I especially hope this book will challenge young Blacks to learn more about their ancestors' cultural contributions to America. We know a lot about others cultures, but many of us lack knowledge about the accomplishments of those early black slaves and others who followed in their footsteps. It is imperative for people to be educated to prevent slavery and other types of oppression from rising again, due to racial prejudice. Cultural contributions have nothing to do with the color of one's skin, but everything to do with the character of one's spirit. A person's identity has much to do with the appreciation of his culture. As a race, Blacks have yet to master this to the same degree as other nationalities. God wants each of us to know our identity so that we can fulfill our destiny.

SIX

Blacks and the Economy

When it comes to economic dreams, people may think Blacks have little interest. However this is not true. This belief may be connected to the apathy that remained after the slave era. During slavery, the slave's only economic contribution was hard work to harvest crops so that his master could have abundant wealth. Those slaves had nothing to add to an already established economy that was focused on hiring cheap labor to increase profit. They had little interest in the economic process, because they had no significant role to play in the American economy. They were strictly laborers.

To them, the term "economy" meant that their clothes, food and shelter were taken care of by their white masters. So, what need would they have had for money? After all, they were not citizens and could not participate in consumer markets. Because they had no identity in the economic system during the slave era, they were not allowed to have money or buy and sell. Neither could they purchase property. If they did have money, what would they have done with it? These were men and women who had not been educated regarding investment and wise money management. Their lives were concerned only with staying physically fit to work the plantation. The economy was their master's duty.

Being deprived of participating in the free enterprise markets left black people ill-equipped to provide anything of value to the economic marketplace. Subsequent to the slave era, Blacks found themselves unprepared to survive within the economic system. Unlike slaves, there were also those free indentured black servants who had been brought to early America who understood the economy of ownership and buying and selling. When they escaped to the North, they had some knowledge of money, property and values. But by-and-large slaves knew nothing about their economy, or did they? Although they were not participants in the free markets, I am confident those slaves dreamed of a place that they could call their own.

Slaves arrived in America from the motherland of Africa, a land of abundant natural resources, a land ruled by kings for centuries before America was even settled. Slaves were imported for the economic benefit of plantation owners, and without this cheap but excellent labor source, the southern economy would have floundered, due to the high cost of labor.

Every successful economy must have producers, sellers, and buyers. Black people became the producers but had no voice in the sale of the products they generated. So, though slaves knew nothing about an advanced economic system, they well understood their responsibility to work hard. This system did guarantee them a form of family stability; as long as the owners made a profit, slave families could stay together, playing an important role in the plantation economy. Thus, it is safe to say that while slaves had no formal education in economics, they did comprehend the survival process. They understood the necessity to work to be retained by their owners, rather than be traded into even more degradation. Ultimately, a sound economy was necessary for the survival of Black family bonds.

It has been said that modern day Blacks define economy as the process of buying and selling. But these days Blacks have a much deeper grasp of the marketing process. Though the world has changed since the slavery era, there remains an exchange system, a market to trade goods and services, and money is the means to purchase them. Unlike the slaves of the past, the average black person today sees the economy as the means to ownership. A slave could own nothing, not even himself. Today, we are blessed to be participants in a free enterprise system. Thus, the economy offers the opportunity to make and spend money, along with owning and operating businesses, and making investments. In spite of the continuing struggle for economic equality, the financial strides of Blacks offer hope for the future, and its effects will ripple forever.

Perhaps it is easier for Blacks to see the effects of a bad economy than to see the immediate effect of a lagging sociology. A sagging economy means the loss of jobs, high prices, unemployment, and pressure on the family structure.

To most black people, a sagging economy means that it will cost more to put food on the table, to pay the mortgage, to get an education, and even to pay church tithes. They are not necessarily concerned with waiting until inflation and high unemployment figures change. Blacks do not understand having to delay putting food on the table so that the economy can correct itself, or for those in power to correct its course. In general, whenever the economy begins to sag, blacks see themselves as the first to suffer the negative fallout. A case in point: I was talking to a Black friend the other day and he remarked, "The economy may be good for some people, but I don't see it yet because the high price of gas and housing has left many of us crippled." He was not saying that the economy had singled out the black people. But since, as a whole, Blacks have lower incomes per household, they typically feel the effects more so than other races. This man understood the economy as more than just selling and purchasing, but as a financial system that affects his quality of life.

Business is a key factor that helps to shape our communities' identities. During slavery, the plantation economy shaped who the slaves were as well as their quality of life. Plantation owners were not interested in the financial future of their slaves, but in profits from crops the slave system produced.

Since the ghetto riots of the sixties, much has been said about how business has influenced the attitude of black communities. America's success will hinge on whether or not it continues to channel business to Blacks, who must have an equal opportunity to participate in the free enterprise system. Failure to pay attention to the economy of the inner cities will eventually have a drastic impact on the economy as a whole. When the economy is healthy across the board, the effect can be seen in the efforts everyone makes to stimulate the markets by investing in our country's future. The economic system must be geared to help those suffering from high prices and escalating costs.

It seems that lately the role of business has been to make fast profit in an atmosphere where financial gain is the only thing that matters. I disagree with that philosophy, because it does not take into consideration how the profit is made. I believe this mentality is detrimental to us as a society and to black people. When making money becomes more important than how it's made, we are on the way to spiritual and moral bankruptcy. I take exception to those who say we have a free enterprise system, and that it is our own business what we charge others for goods and services. Such an "anything goes" attitude occurs when we build an economy on profiteering and not on Christian principles regarding how we accumulate our assets. I believe that in order for an economy to see the lasting blessings of God, it must be based on a responsive spirit. This is the spirit that does not focus upon profit alone, but on how that profit is made.

I remember reading the work of an author who believed that "Black capitalism" rings a responsive chord with many businesses and congressional leaders. He did not think that "Black capitalism" alone was a solution to what troubles the ghetto and lower income Blacks. He didn't think it mattered whose capital it was as long as it promoted area development. On the other hand some will argue that it is very important to the black community and its economic identity if area investors are Black or mostly Black. This group feels that it does much for Blacks living in impoverished areas to see that fellow successful Blacks have not forgotten their struggling brothers. Knowing that a black person owns a local business directly affects the pride and dignity of the black community. Black investors can then encourage other Blacks to get on board and support programs that respond to the needs of black neighborhoods. In other words, they want to see investors who can relate and identify with the struggles of the black community.

By providing capital, training and markets, some white businessmen inspire black entrepreneurs to invest in their own communities. Still, black capitalism has had its disappointments for both White and Black investors. Thus far, White-sponsored efforts to help with this capital problem have failed. Black leaders acknowledge that they want to be their own bosses and believe they should receive more aid. And some aren't sure black-owned businesses will employ enough of their own people or generate enough wealth to make a significant difference. The plight of a people and its economic mystique is a very complicated matter. Several factors contribute to the economic struggles black people face today. We have already discussed the after effects of the slave era, and the impoverished imprints it left behind.

During the riots of the sixties, government programs were instituted to bring about black ownership in the financial arena. Notwithstanding this, many black-owned businesses failed because there were insufficient funds to maintain export capital, to develop credit and promote black ownership in the core areas. Thus, any future plan will have to encourage equal opportunity loans for everyone regardless of race or sex. Banks and credit lenders should be encouraged to approve loans to black investors just as any other race or nationality.

The inner city areas need additional capital to enable them to participate in the investment markets. They do not need discouragement, but positive investment role models from every race. Since it is clear that the current economy stifles the possibility of creating wealth and ownership of productive capital, we must develop and seek to establish new methodologies to attract investors in the black communities.

Black neighborhoods desperately need the support of the independent sector to join government-sponsored programs to improve the economy of black neighborhoods. In a simple sense, associations and clubs, both private and public, have something to offer black neighborhoods. The independent sector needs to train Blacks to think more about long-term investment markets and relationships. Some independent and private sector organizations believe that inner city conditions are the way they are because of all the welfare people living there. In other words, they believe Blacks enjoy living in poverty. Historically, many of our independent sector sponsors have been paternalistic. By this,

I mean they paid the bills for poor black people but never really focused on equipping them to take care of themselves by independent initiatives. A few have refused such methods and managed to provide assistance while encouraging the poor to help themselves. These groups too have often suffered from internal failures that caused them to be, for the most part, ineffective. The efforts of the independent sector, to a large extent, suffer the same fate as many government efforts to conquer the evils of poverty. Cutbacks in funding also kill many programs.

This argument should not result in protests against the government or against independent sector programs. Protests and finger-pointing will not generate funds to help low-income black neighborhoods. We must come to face the situation as it is, and everyone must do what they can to further the community's involvement in the economy. What would be most helpful is if investment organizations would offer their expertise and investment strategies to help turn the tide in the long term.

Perhaps the most effective approach would be to offer incentives for wealthy investors to stop investing all capital profits in the suburbs and to work more with the black communities to spearhead self-help programs. Some of these ideas are already being implemented today. There are positive indications that such an approach will be effective in the long term.

Another factor that has significantly impacted the black economy is elected government officials. Most black people tend to believe that Democrats are more likely to represent the economic programs that will benefit them, and programs that address the economic plight of black people and the poor. The average black person sees a direct correlation between the economic opportunities available and who is in the White House or in Congress. Past history seems to confirm that Republicans are more likely to support programs attractive to big business. This trend has won the Republican Party the support of most big business organizations. On the other hand, there is a tendency for the Democratic Party to support and sponsor social programs that will help those at the lower socio-economic levels.

Blacks believe that when Democrats are in office, they are more likely to be heard. They believe these officials will improve the conditions that matter most to them. The significance of this perception is that if the wrong individual is elected to office, Blacks feel that they are going to be the first to feel the effects that will likely take years to overcome. Since the Republican Party programs direct their aims in different directions to improve the economy, black people in general do not register and vote for Republicans. The average Black believes that the person elected to the presidency has much to do with his economic plight. Whether true or not, this is the general position of the Black race as a whole.

While I believe this may be a notable trend, I am inclined to believe that other factors created and endorsed by Blacks have an even more profound impact on the economic plight of the average black person. To a large extent, it is up to Blacks to change their outlook toward earning and spending income and investment strategies. It is easy for us to blame the Caucasian race for the economic destiny of black people. The Caucasian race is not responsible for all the problems Blacks face in search of their economic identity. It is true that there are problems with the way leadership handles the economy that tend to injure black people more than others. But all the responsibility should not be laid at their feet.

I believe the primary responsibility might lie with us as Blacks. I am a Black American male who, for years has observed us going the wrong way, heading away from the very same God who's been urging us to return to the thinking and attitude of our ancestors. What do I mean by that? For decades now, we have been mistaken about who to blame for the economic struggles of the black race.

For example, when was the last time you read a how-to book about wise money management? When was the last time you sat down to explain to your children about investing wisely and being careful with their money?

Before writing this book, I spent time asking Blacks these questions, and I was not surprised by their answers. Most admitted to being too busy to do much research on how to save and govern their spending habits. The average black household spends too much on things that will do little to help improve their economic position, and they will not allow God to define who they are and their role in the larger U.S. economy. As a whole, Blacks feel they are too busy or don't have the funds to save and invest.

But how valid are these arguments? Not as valid as we might think. The first problem is directly linked to our thinking and spending habits. No matter how much we try to understand the financial struggles of Blacks, we must come clean and admit we have not done enough to address the problems that plague us.

Perhaps the greatest problem we as adults must address is the way we ourselves spend and invest. Younger generations learn from us. If we practice better spending and earning habits, members of the younger generation are much more likely to apply them to their own lives.

I was at work the other day when I had a conversation with two Black professionals. We were discussing the current economic problems facing the Black race. I asked this question, "Why do you think we as a people have such a poor financial foundation?" My companions felt that Blacks were held back and could do nothing to help themselves. I listened to how discrimination has hindered the Black race. In reality, I could not disagree with their arguments. As a race, black people have always had lower paying jobs, made less money, and have been denied loans necessary for investing in business.

Their reasons had nothing to do with what we as a race needed to do, but what others needed to change. I totally agreed that changes should be made to strengthen Black financial markets. However, I was more inclined than they to say that these were not the only problems. I asked, "But how about our own failures to correct our financial situations?" Then, I said "Let me explain what I'm talking about." I continued, "While we might not be able to correct external factors, we definitely can change the internal factors that impact our personal finances." My point was that we must stop our shallow thinking and start thinking deep about long-term plans and goals.

I would dare say that too few black persons spend time making long-term goals that could improve their own financial situation, and would eventually, affect the entire black race. In general, the average working-class black person focuses on the short term instead of planning ahead.

During slavery, the slaves had no choice but to think short-term because they were denied the freedom to improve their economic plight. But is this our problem today? Most would agree that whereas our ancestors had no alternatives, you and I have the ability to improve our situation. I am not including those Blacks that are confined to the ghetto areas with no hope of tomorrow. But even here, it's true that many poor people spend most of their income on things with no value. I have read several reports within the past few days that confirm this fact. Even our sisters and brothers who work in low-paying jobs do not plan ahead and start slowly working their way out of their situations. In many cases, there may be no instant way out. But poor people must also dream, making a long-term plan for improving their circumstances, even a little at a time. They must think more along the line of saving for tomorrow and not spending the little they have for today, leaving nothing for the future. Unfortunately, for many black families who barely make ends meet, saving is merely a dream.

So where do we fail to spend wisely? We are unwise each time we spend money for a car we cannot afford. I am reminded of a man who told me he was going to buy a new automobile. I asked, "What kind of car are you going to buy?" He replied, "Oh I'm not going to buy just any car, but one I've always wanted." I asked, "What kind is that?" He immediately replied, "I've always wanted a Cadillac, and since I've caught up paying my bills, this is an excellent time to do it." I asked, "Do you have enough money in the bank to pay your mortgage and other bills for the next six-months should something happen to you?" He answered, "Charles, I'm not thinking about paying bills six months down the road." He continued, "All my life I wanted to get myself a Caddy, and I've made up my mind to get it." When he didn't answer my question I knew he was not thinking long term. Many of us think only about paying our bills and debts that are due today. It is almost as if we are immune to the long-term possibilities of the distant future.

Because we might not live to see the future, it is a gross mistake not to plan for it. Even if we refuse to think in terms of twenty-year goals, it is immature to not plan to cover our household expenses and debts for a twelve-month period. Think about this for a moment. God forbid, but just suppose you become ill or suddenly die. How will your family make it? Have you provided any resources for them to live on in your absence? I am appalled at the number of us Blacks who live from paycheck to paycheck. Many of these are middle class professionals. Few give enough consideration to what might happen to us or our families.

The young man I mentioned above never said a word about the consequences of his decision to purchase that expensive automobile. A failure on our part to think before making hasty decisions will, in the end, cause heartache for our grieving families should we become ill or die. Unfortunately for the young man who bought his dream car, less than two years later he became ill, and his mortgage became delinquent. He eventually lost both his home and the Cadillac. It was sad that he had to learn the hard way what happens when we live for the moment.

Blacks and other minorities tend to spend money they do not have. At times we purchase temporal things like video games and cell phones for ourselves and our children, but do not plan for long-term goals and survival. I can remember when cell phones were a luxury item. Now, almost every ten-year-old owns one. I wonder how many parents thought about taking that money to start a savings account for the child's future.

I am well aware that some parents buy cell phones for emergencies. But let's be real for a moment; how many times have their children had emergencies, and how often have the cell phones been used to socialize with their friends or for other purposes? In fact, reports confirm that phones are very often used to sell drugs and arrange dates during school hours. While there is nothing innately wrong with having a cell phone, we need to ask ourselves if a phone purchase was a wise decision in the long term. Will the cell phone cause Johnny to use his money wisely? Will it help him to plan for his future? The monthly recurring phone charges are also obligations that must be met. Would not this money be better spent if it had been placed in a savings or investment fund for Johnny's college tuition?

We often purchase athletic shoes for our children, even though they already have three or four pairs. The reason that I bring this up is because I had a friend who is a single mother and at one time her son was purchasing a different pair of shoes for every day of the week. When she spoke to me, she complained about her son's tendency to buy more shoes when he already had several pairs. She could not understand the wisdom in this and yet she bought them for her son. Now, you tell me, does this make any sense at all? One day when she was especially frustrated with her son, I asked, "Why don't you stop paying for those shoes and take him to the bank or somewhere to start a saving or investment fund?" She replied, "That won't add up to much." But then I said to her, "I know that it won't immediately add up to much of a savings account, just several hundred a year." The reason I said that was because at the time those shoes were costing more than a hundred dollars a pair. It doesn't take a rocket scientist to see that a thousand dollars spent in tennis shoes that would be worn and discarded could be better deposited for the young man's education. What struck me most was that the mother could see no long-term benefits in training her son to invest wisely and to save his money. In this case, it was her money being spent and wasted and he had no stake in the matter.

This is not a rare incident but happens frequently. We fuss and complain about our children wasting money, and yet we are the ones financing the spending sprees. So, I ask you, who is at fault here? I would say that we as parents are to blame because we supply the money while failing to teach the importance of long-term goals and delayed gratification. I believe we could go into the average Black American home and find shelves of video games and expensive equipment on which to play them. I'm convinced that the practice of buying temporal material things for our children will lead them to think and live only for the moment. They will be focused on pleasure and entertainment, unable to restrain their desires. We must ask ourselves-are we not truly partially responsible for the teenagers who grow up in life unprepared to handle the realities of survival?

Although none of us want our children to be deprived, we must pause to think about the long-term effect that such temporal thinking will have on their future. We are sending a strong message to our children that they can have what they want without waiting or making any kind of sacrifice. Then, we wonder why Charlie doesn't demonstrate responsibility? Simply put, we cannot allow our children to grow up thinking that material things will define their identity. The truth is, these things actually detract from the real person God intended for them to be. Identity is not acquired from owning things, but from getting to know the one that cares for and loves us. There is a grave danger for our contemporary black society when we try to get our identity from any source other than a personal relationship with the Lord Jesus Christ. We continue to buy these young people the latest fads and fashions, and they keep wandering further away from feeling complete in life, because they don't have a personal relationship with Jesus Christ.

We model economic planning by purchasing things that do not represent wisdom, patience and maturity. These temporal things will not show future generations how to prepare a budget for their households or take care of their families. Neither will they teach them the importance of making wise decisions when it is time to decide what and how to purchase those things that yield the best return for the future.

During slavery, Blacks had no access to the better things of life, and had no reason to focus on good financial planning. In our contemporary black society, many of us find ourselves desiring too many material things. While there is nothing intrinsically wrong with having nice things, the pursuit of such things can be devastating because we focus on things more than on God. When this happens we are less likely to make wise economic decisions for ourselves and our families, as has been the case with many black families. A failure to implement sound financial planning with spiritual wisdom leads one to purchase expensive things without the resources to fund them. As a Black race, this is exactly where many of us find ourselves. This becomes a self-fulfilling prophecy when we spend money beyond our means, knowing we are gambling against the future to secure the present.

So, what are some results of our poor spending habits? When we adopt irresponsible spending practices we are more likely to find our closets full of unworn clothes, many of them with price tags still attached. In many cases, we have worn them just once or twice, before they lose their appeal. Some of these clothes should never have been purchased, because we already had a closet bulging with adequate clothing. I'm sure that if each of us takes a close look into our closets, we will find things that were too expensive, where the money could have been better spent on things with a higher long-term yield. In fact, many of us have an overabundance of clothes we will never wear. After a time, they will be discarded and the money invested in them also discarded. You know this is the truth.

If we are honest, we would have to admit we waste money on unnecessary or overly expensive apparel. I recently examined the contents of my own closet and noticed all the shirts I have that I've never worn. However, I have no intention of discarding them until I have gotten more wear out of them. Obviously, there is no need for me to buy shirts or receive them as gifts. I truly believe that upon visiting most Black American homes, we would see many new and unworn clothes in the closets.

As a matter of fact, I recently went to visit a sick member of our church, and when I arrived, there were shoes everywhere—over fifty pairs of shoes, as well as dozens of shirts and suits. All that money spent to fill that walk-in closet. I decided right then that I would make others aware of the excessive amounts we as a people spend on clothing. I am not saying that God does not want us to be blessed with changes of clothes, but I believe we are overdoing it.

Instead of investing this money for the future, we purchase temporary items that will produce nothing in the long run. And if men are doing this, it's probable that women are as well, especially because they tend to frequent shopping malls. Chances are that the majority of these purchases are really not necessary. I challenge lower and middle class Blacks to inspect the surplus of garments hanging in their closets. We could alleviate much of our economic struggle if we would learn to resist buying on impulse. In other words, we need to stop shopping "sales" that encourage us to purchase on credit whatever our hearts desire.

My question is, "Could we not have done without this purchase?" Should not we have put the $150.00 spent on those additional clothes in a savings or investment account? Then, what about the interest charges on those items we purchase with credit? The point I'm making is this: that we are wasting money on depreciating items instead of investing in our future. Impulse buying is a major problem within the Afro-American community. Purchasing should be planned and evaluated to determine whether it is in line with God's plan for our lives.

Not only are we as a race spending wastefully on temporal things like clothes, video games and cell phones, but we mistakenly believe our identity is tied to the size of our homes, our glamour appeal, and the price of our cars. This kind of spending undermines the very foundation of who we are as a race and a nation. Many Black women spend far too much on clothes, makeup and expensive jewelry. And while jewelry deals can be a type of investment, we have to be honest with ourselves, are we really thinking "investment" when we purchase jewelry? How much jewelry do we have at home that is serving no investment purpose at all? For most of us, such things are status symbols. If women are honest with themselves they will have to admit that many of the jewelry bills they face today are the result of frivolous spending, and the money could have been more wisely used elsewhere.

You may be thinking "I don't believe that." Well, let me back up my statements with facts. On occasion I have counseled black couples with marital problems, and finances were a major part of the problem. In each case, the wife had spent far too much on expensive jewelry, which they readily admitted was a mistake. Not only this, the past week while traveling for my job I had a conversation with a black female that I have known for some time, and we discussed getting out of debt so that retirement would not be so stressful. I replied, "Most of us waste money on things we could have lived without." She replied, "You know, Charles, you're right. As I look back I confess I've struggled to pay bills for jewelry I never should've bought."

She continued, "I purchased a ring that cost several thousand dollars because I was depressed and thought it would make me feel better." She added, "If the store manager hadn't humiliated me by asking if I as a black woman could afford this ring, I probably would not have gone through with the deal." As a result, she ran up an unnecessary bill that took over five years to pay off. I commended her for her honesty. Many of us will continue to make bad purchasing decisions because we do not understand our mistakes. I thank God that this woman had learned from her mistakes, and chances are she will not repeat them.

In the same way, black men tend to buy exorbitantly expensive vehicles. Earlier I mentioned a gentleman who purchased an expensive Cadillac because it made him feel good about himself. No doubt, most of us know others who purchased vehicles because it made them feel good. I often notice all the new and expensive vehicles that go in and out of my own neighborhood, and many are luxury cars with high price tags. I am not saying these folks should not purchase nice cars, but perhaps instead of spending close to $40,000, it would have been wiser to purchase a vehicle that cost $30,000 and then save or invest the other $10,000 toward long-term goals. Obviously we believe a more expensive vehicle will earn us a more distinguished identity.

In other words, such a purchase will cause folks to look up to us with envy, which makes us believe we've arrived.

Many Blacks purchase overly expensive homes in search of their individual identity. I remember a conversation I had with a man seeking to buy another house, and I encouraged him to pray and use godly wisdom before making the purchase. This person replied, "Oh, we'll have God's blessing because He's promised to give me what my heart desires." His reasoning was, "God wants me to have the biggest and best." And because his theology was messed up, he went on to purchase a massive, expensive dream home, which was way beyond his budget. And while there was nothing innately wrong with his desire for a nice home, he acted unwisely, and it wasn't long before his income was unable to accommodate the payments. Needless to say, years later he lost that home and had to downsize to an apartment, losing his shirt in the deal. So the question is: Did God forsake him when he needed Him most? No, but God wants us to find our identity in Jesus Christ and not in what we own.

The search for identity has led many Blacks to become victims of the bankruptcy monster. If we do not take control of our spending, we will eventually be led into bankruptcy. Many have no intention of having to file for bankruptcy or being forgiven debts they themselves incurred. While some may believe that people who file bankruptcy just want to take advantage of the system, I'm not convinced this defines the large majority of those who declare bankruptcy. Continuous unwise spending practices ultimately leave them no other choice. The sad thing is that even after trying to encourage Blacks not to overspend, our race tends to ignore wisdom and continues to march toward bankruptcy. We feel compelled to hide the truth from our peers, unwilling for them to know our true financial state. In the end, however, the truth comes out.

Though this may sound ridiculous, it is reality. Over the years, I have counseled many struggling Blacks who had deceived their peers, pretending they were on top of their deteriorating financial situations. Instead of making necessary drastic changes in a timely manner, they spent more.

Several years ago, some married friends of ours found themselves in financial trouble. My wife, who is skilled at helping others to budget, counseled and advised them on how to turn the situation around. But instead of following wisdom, they resumed spending beyond their means, simply to impress their peers. And while the husband continually cautioned his wife about adhering to the budget, his wife convinced him otherwise and eventually they were back in trouble again. Needless to say before long they had no choice but to declare bankruptcy, and they never recovered from the disaster.

People go to great lengths to prevent others from learning about their financial difficulty. I am not saying that any of us should advertise our financial predicaments, but we jeopardize our future when we insist on "keeping up with the Joneses," and then covering it up.

Some years ago, I had another associate of mine who also ended up having to file for bankruptcy. Early on she knew that both their finances and their marriage were in trouble. She said that no matter how much she tried to convince her husband that they were operating beyond their incomes, he would not listen. He would host family gatherings and go on vacations they could not afford. She was responsible for the family budget, but did not get the cooperation necessary to prevent bankruptcy. Not long after returning from a vacation, she had to take drastic steps to keep them from losing everything they owned, and eventually they filed for bankruptcy. The husband became upset arguing that if she had been wiser in managing their spending, they could have stopped the downward spiral. He had forgotten her repeated warnings about their rapidly deteriorating financial situation. When everything began to go sour, he finally recognized they were in trouble, but in the end, he couldn't understand how things had gone bad.

I know of other black families who earned middle to upper level incomes and were doing well, until unwise spending eventually led them into bankruptcy and divorce court. A wise man will take instruction to preserve his life and credit, because bankruptcy irreparably harms both our reputation and credit and often leaves us blaming others rather than assuming responsibility for our actions.

Black economic problems are the result of several factors. Some are beyond our control with regard to job discrimination because of race, but many could be eliminated entirely by adhering to the principles of the Word of God. Scripture tells us God wants us to prosper and be in good health, but we must live according to God's Word to receive His promises and blessings. This means no one can rebel against God spiritually and financially and expect to inherit God's promises. Blacks will probably always have to face certain hindrances that other races will not, but they must remember that in Philippians 4:19, God promised to supply their needs if they obey his commands and live wisely.

This promise does not mean we can do whatever we want and expect His blessing. While God does have unlimited resources, He knows that an undisciplined life leads to self-destruction, as in the case of most bankruptcies. And as we examine our spiritual walk, we may be surprised what we find. A person with undisciplined spending habits also lives an undisciplined spiritual life. To receive God's richest blessings in all areas of our lives, we must discipline ourselves and our children, and learn to live according to the Word of God.

Slavery undoubtedly left deep scars on the black culture, but God heals. However, we must not add new scars by living undisciplined lives that bring financial disaster. Buying our identity with money and things may make us feel important for a while, but this feeling is temporary. As black parents we need to train our children to be content with what they have—to wait and work hard for what they want. And we must encourage them to be cautious about the danger of excessive wants. But, before we can do that, we need to learn to delay our own gratification. Children need to see the Word of God in action through their parents' actions. God promised to supply all our needs, but not necessarily all our wants. We often forget this fact and begin to pursue material things. Adam and Eve's wants brought sin into the Garden of Eden after they failed to obey the specific instructions of God.

Afro Americans must not enslave themselves by buying things that have no lasting value. Unfortunately, many of the well known entertainment heroes have found financial success, but their lives remain blatant examples of misuse of fame and fortune, with no thought of living surrendered lives to God. Even many Christians believe that they can live financial reckless and undisciplined lives and still be blessed by God. Success can become a form of idol worshiping. God instructs us that we are to worship him and only him. Our identity and feelings of self-worth only come from a personal relationship with Jesus Christ. The Bible tells us to seek the Kingdom of God, and all these other things He will add unto us. If we seek to establish our identity with material things, they will be our master. But when we identify with heavenly things and the will and purpose of God, then He will take care of us. We as black people must learn to live within our means. Unwise spending habits cause many of our dire financial circumstances, and we cannot expect God or anyone else to magically fix them for us.

At Christmas time I've been appalled by shopping carts I see heavily laden with things that will be forgotten only days later. I wonder when we will learn that purchasing gifts does nothing to put money in the bank or keep our debts under control.

Instead of attending church, becoming saved, and paying our tithes, too many of us, including those that can least afford not to, refuse to come to Jesus where we might layup treasures in heaven instead of on earth. . We must start today to seek our economic identity from Jesus Christ. He said come; we do not need money to buy from Him; His love is free and available to all.

Across the board, we as black people need to examine our spending habits to see if they are in line with God's Word. We will never be content in God or know who we are until our priorities line up with God's purpose and plan. When a man surrenders his life to Christ, he is on the way to finding his identity, because he knows money and things do not define him; only salvation and allowing God to live His life through us will fill the emptiness inside. Perhaps our black slave ancestors did not have the things we have today, but they understood better than many of us the real source of their identity.

SEVEN

Blacks and the Crime Scene

John F. Kennedy once said, "Those who make peaceful revolutions impossible make violent revolutions inevitable." This is a loaded statement, but more importantly it is true. The time has come for every American to consider the meaning of this statement. If we stand against peaceful means to resolve conflict, then we may inadvertently support violent measures. Crime and violence are a problem threatening not only Blacks, but also our nation.

What does the term "crime" means? It means to commit a deviant offense against someone or against the state. At one time, the United States was a peaceful and tranquil place. But something happened, and now peace is only a distant memory. "Crime and violence," "law and order," and "justice" have become phrases we discuss. Crime seems to have become a crippling part of Americans lives. We are no longer a nation of peace, and criminal activity continues to rise in the inner cities and suburbs. It is commonly believed that Blacks are responsible for most criminal behavior-But is this fact or myth?

According to court statistics, more Blacks than Whites enter the justice system before being convicted and sentenced to prison.

Theories about Crime

There are numerous theories about crime, each having some validity. One such premise is based on the theory of opportunity that says crimes are committed primarily because of the imbalance in opportunities available to different segments of society. If legitimate means do not bring desired gain, then illegal means will suffice. Some researchers believe this theory explains the rationale behind property crimes. They assert that black people commit more property crimes than other races because of their lack of opportunity to obtain things through legal means. And while there may be some validity to this theory, I am not convinced this is the truth. The lack of opportunity does not give us the right to violate the will of God. I strongly support the principle that no one should take that which he does not legally own. The Word of God says: "Thou shall not steal." Taking what does not belong to us will ultimately bring the wrath of God upon us. We need only to look at the overcrowded prison system that is filled with Blacks to see the consequences of adhering to this theory. We cannot find our identity using ungodly means.

A second theory says Black crime is a social condition resulting from a lack of norms. This theory is based on the belief that crime stems from a lack of consistent rules to govern the members within a subculture. Its solution must then be aimed at equalizing rules to apply across the board.

Let's examine how this applies to crime in the black population. . This theory sees Blacks as having experienced a different set of rules dating back to the slavery era. Supporters of this theory believe that throughout history society made laws primarily aimed at black people. This effort was met with resistance, and Blacks soon discovered that the law was unequally enforced depending on the race of the offender.

They contend that Blacks responded by inventing their own code of ethics to survive within white society. Another theory espoused by some crime experts is that socioeconomic status is the greatest determining factor for

Blacks in the justice system. Evidence has shown that socioeconomics is an important determinant of who is prosecuted and who is not. Additionally, evidence indicates race has also played a part in determining punishment over the past 250 years. Clearly, both race and money, or the lack thereof, contributes greatly in the determination of the fate of Blacks in the criminal justice system.

Stereotyping is another theory experts use to explain the high proportion of crimes committed by the Black race. Those who advocate this theory believe that assigning racial stereotypes tends to become a self-fulfilling prophecy. In other words, when we label Black people as more violent or more likely to steal, they live up to the standard we have set. When this is the case, law enforcement officials become more suspicious of black people and are more likely to arrest them with very little cause.

While the various theories discussed above may help us understand Blacks and crime, we must be cautious in using a single theory to explain deviant behavior in any race. We must first understand that criminal behavior has been around since the beginning of time, as explained in the Bible. Cain slew his brother Abel. God disapproved of Cain's crime back then, and he still disapproves of those who use crime to resolve conflicts. Crime is a problem not unique to Blacks, but because it is sin that separates the sinner from God, it is a societal problem that affects everyone.

Relationship of Blacks and Law Enforcement Officers

What is the relationship between Blacks and law enforcement? In general, how do the police and black people view each other? Some Blacks perceive themselves as targets of law enforcement and the justice system. They look upon all law enforcement officials with suspicion. On the other end of the scale, there are many law enforcement officials who view Blacks with ambivalence and prejudice. In this case, perhaps Blacks and law enforcement officials are both victims of stereotyping and resentment, not only because of how they feel toward each other, but also how society feels toward them in general. Blacks are too often cast as automatically having criminal tendencies, and Blacks automatically believe that law enforcement officers use extreme methods when dealing with them in an attempt to keep order.

From the early slavery years, Blacks viewed law enforcement officers with much suspicion and resentment. They did so because of the force used to suppress Blacks and keep them in "their place." During the slavery era, white officers patrolled the cities insuring that no runaways were allowed to enter cities to be transported to the North. When they were able to read, slaves read historical references that detailed the role law enforcement officers played in enforcing slavery. This left a bitter resentment in their minds. Thus both law officers and Blacks became victims of the system.

There is probably no more vivid picture of the struggle between law enforcement officials and Blacks than the riots of the sixties and seventies. During that time, America experienced hatred and resentment that left a terrible scar. When law enforcement officers were called to enforce the laws, protecting society as a whole, they were caught in the middle, forced to go head-to-head with Blacks, thus creating enemies.

While many officers enjoyed their work and believed they were just doing their jobs, many Blacks were offended. To them, the law enforcement officers were perpetuating the very injustices their ancestors had been subjected to during the slavery era. Many Blacks today still believe laws and law enforcement officers exist to keep them in their place.

There is evidence to suggest an affinity between police work and support for radical-right politics. During the sixties, George Wallace was considered a hero by many southern police officers. He was endorsed by the largest police organization in America and frequently referred to the heroic activities of the police, denouncing Supreme Court decisions as well as other "bleeding heart liberals," for undermining police efforts to maintain order. As a result, law enforcement officials were viewed as soldiers for the establishment, while Blacks became known as anti-establishment.

Throughout the history of politics, law enforcement officers have largely supported conservative candidates for office. In general, they were viewed as opposed to the civil rights and integration movements. As a result, many police officers instigated political action to stop integration and did what they could to discourage school integration. Studies concluded that law enforcement officials in general, endorsed "political conservatism," blocking efforts to keep Blacks from societal equality. But is this belief substantiated by fact?

According to history books, there is evidence to support this position; most conservative societies have been supported by law enforcement officials. Although there is an unofficial rule that law enforcement must be politically neutral when enforcing the law, this has not always been the case. Many law enforcement officials have been active in organizations such as the John Birch Society and Ku Klux Klan group.

Researchers conducted studies to evaluate police attitudes in the South, proving that the majority held deep-seated anti-black sentiment. . Blacks reasoned that societal pressure had convinced the average police officer to despise and hate them.

With a better grasp of history, we can see why Blacks rebel against law enforcement. But we can no longer afford to rationalize criminal behavior and hold on to feelings of hatred and hostility. Blacks must change the way they look at law enforcement, learning to respect officers charged with enforcing the laws and upholding justice for everyone, regardless of race. Crime is a problem that affects everyone. No matter how we attempt to explain high crime rates within the Black race, unanswered questions will remain. Setting high moral standards to eradicate the stigma of crime upon the image of the black people will do much to improve their identity.

Juveniles and Crime

Another area we must address is juvenile behavior in the Black community. Juvenile crime rates are steadily rising. The crime problem actually originates with juveniles, who have displayed criminal behavior from childhood. Though some are first time offenders the majority are repeat offenders who have gotten caught in the juvenile court system as children and teens. And unless effective treatment methods are administered, they will languish and eventually perish in the penal system.

It used to be that juvenile crimes were petty infractions that could be resolved by simple means. Today, this has drastically changed and young Blacks are getting caught up in more sophisticated and dangerous types of crimes. Many commit offenses that demand they be adjudicated by the adult prison system. Unless they receive early counseling to turn their lives around, it is highly likely that they will end up in prison.

Over the years, I have read a number of books about young men and women who somehow got involved with the wrong crowd. One book written by Claude Brown, entitled, *Man Child in a Promise Land*, detailed how he ended up in the criminal subculture. As a young boy, I became fascinated with the author's story. Terrible problems led to this young man's gang-controlled life.

It's high time to address the problem of gangs, who are responsible for a great deal of the juvenile crime in Black neighborhoods. The gang is a criminal subculture that preys upon those with a need to belong. As a youth, Claude Brown sought out the gang to help him survive a very hard life, and he found a group who claimed it would love and care for him. At least one in every five crimes committed are gang-related. To many young Blacks, gangs represent a new found family, a place to belong. In fact, the gang may become a parent to many of its members. They are usually made up of children and teens who have no special niche and no one to love them. Thus, the gang subculture becomes a place where they fit in. In this case, a bad niche is better than no niche at all. They do not care that this is a violent and criminal subculture, only that it is a place they can call home, with friends they can identify with as family.

When I read Brown's book, I was amazed at how all-encompassing the juvenile gang subculture can be to those seeking love and protection. Years have come and gone since then, but Brown's story makes perfect sense. He could count on the safety of the gang when he needed protection from retaliation. Though filled with dangerous delinquents, the gang replaced his family support system. It became the means to survive in the criminal world, where only the strong survive, as in the "survival of the fittest." What intrigued me most about Brown's story was that he grew up in a family with parents who were often too busy trying to keep clothes on his back and a roof over his head to address his emotional needs. Nothing has changed today. Gangs still fill the need to belong.

During my senior year in college, I served an internship at one of the local juvenile institutions. I was assigned to counsel a young man who, like Brown, had lived within the gang subculture, though he had grown up with both parents and a solid value system. His gang was structured so members could survive in a world where exploitation was the norm. When I listened to him talk about gang life it took my breath away. He was a slightly built young man and not very muscular, but he boasted that his gang protected him. It made him feel very secure, knowing protection was there if he needed it. He was thirteen when he served in the gang, which had members up to age twenty-four. His story was intriguing; how could he have gotten caught up in a gang subculture after coming from a solid two-parent home? For one thing, he grew up in a ghetto where criminal behavior was accepted and ignored. To cope with his environment, he joined a gang and gained an identity. From his point of view, gang membership was simply a way to survive, not just rebellion for its own sake.

From him I learned that all gang behavior depends upon the leadership of two or three members. Each member must be loyal and an asset, contributing something to the survival of the group, or he will be expelled.

Interesting enough, those young people who are caught up in the gang subculture really want to contribute something to society but have no role model to show them the way.

As strange as it sounds, these kids yearn to belong, and most remain loyal to the death. Many black youths are crying out to be accepted, to be part of something they can belong to and identify with. Unfortunately, many turn to the criminal subculture to find acceptance, and the tragedy of this is that they become more interested in pursuing a life that actually hinders them from obtaining acceptance. As we have seen, gangs attract those who need to belong; they provide a way to become someone special in a world that has forgotten they exist. Within many black communities gangs dominate and often determine the amount of criminal behavior that occurs there. Gangs give each member a chance to acquire status he may never have experienced before, a chance to develop a personal identity. For many, this is the first time they've been told that they have something significant to contribute toward life. It is this new identity that causes the individual to desire to belong and become actively involved in criminal behavior. Many young black gang members are in search of an identity that is both rewarding and promising.

Gangs exist to survive for the present only. If members cannot provide what they seek, membership will be short-lived. For a while, they enjoy a new identity and a deep sense of loyalty, secrets, cohesiveness and brotherhood. This sense of belonging offers something that material possessions cannot give, but belonging comes at a terrible price—often the cost of their lives. God alone can provide them with the identity and sense of belonging they seek.

In conversations with my counselee, I learned that his decision to join was his own, but once a member he stayed because he felt significant. Perhaps in our search to understand why street gangs persist we should understand the needs they address.

As in Claude Brown's book, this young man explained to me the importance of parents, especially black parents taking time early in life to talk with their children about the yearning to belong and help them to understand that gangs cannot permanently satisfy their emotional or spiritual needs.. I believe today's young people join gangs because we fail to help them understand who they really are. As a result, they go through life seeking someone to fill that void. This young man described in minute detail the life of each member of his gang and how gang membership guaranteed survival in their crime-ridden neighborhoods. On the other hand, non-membership left a youth alone and terribly vulnerable. In fact, not belonging to the gang increased chances for an early death.

While the gang controlled my counselee's life, it also created purpose for living. When I grasped the importance of the gang in imparting identity, I realized most Black parents are far too late when we finally address these kinds of issues with our kids. They need to know from early ages that they were created especially by God for his good pleasure and purpose (Phil. 2:13).

Today, more than ever, black youth are being drawn into street gangs in their search for belonging. Their lives are empty, and they have no hope for the future. Within the gang, there is a strength and cohesiveness that entraps young people who get involved strictly for attention and someone to love them. Once they have been alienated and left outside positive societal groups, they become more vulnerable to the influence of gangs. We must be aware that street gangs exist, and they have become a delinquent subsystem that encompasses every socioeconomic level. Such gangs are producing hardened young black males that most likely will enter the adult penal systems unless they receive some form of intervention counseling.

In the minds of many poor Blacks of the ghetto, they have little hope for change. Their lives are difficult and exhausting, just trying to make ends meet. Because of this, children often do not receive personal attention and encouragement. The gang provides a false sense of security and identity to children starving for love and positive self-actualization. It attracts those who do not know God and know nothing of His unconditional love.

Every person has an innate need to belong to a loving and all-wise God. Unless black parents introduce their small children to the real love of Jesus Christ, they will continue to seek their identity in street gangs and their peers.

If I have learned anything out of my college intern study, it is that many of us as black parents fail to help our children learn their importance to us and to God. In a world where things move at a rapid pace, there are those who are left behind. And when this happens, they are vulnerable to the draw of the gang. Both Claude Brown and my counselee felt rejected by their parents and the very society that was supposed to reinforce their sense of belonging. They found a place to call home in the gang, where they could come and be themselves, even though they were being destroyed.

It is my hope that we can learn how to counteract the gang influence in society. Our young teenagers depend on us to protect them from the criminal elements of society, but too often we send them there. We are too busy chasing money to teach our children who they are in God. Instead, we model materialism that will ultimately, leave them feeling worthless and alone.

For a long time, street gangs had little influence in affluent neighborhoods, but this has changed. Well-to-do teenagers seek identity and belonging in the same way as those in ghettos. Unless they receive a sense of belonging from their parents and other family members they are prone to look elsewhere. The earlier we educate our children to the truth of God's love, the less likely they are to become a part of the criminal scene.

I can think of no better way to explain the problem of crime in black communities than to explain how such problems are rooted in early childhood. When I grew up as a kid, crime and delinquency was almost unheard of in my community. But as I grew older, things began to change and so did crime and delinquency. But then social values began to erode and opportunism began to flourish. In many respects, crime became a new means to reach one's goals. I am not saying there was no crime in our neighborhood, but during my early teen years, I knew no one who had been arrested for a crime. The worst thing that ever happened was a fight between two drunks on the weekend. Weapons were never used to retaliate against an enemy. During my early teenage years, I can honestly say that I knew of no cases of murder or even property crimes. Maybe we were sheltered, but we learned to live peacefully with all men, if at all possible.

However, during my late teens, I noticed a shift in the trends of criminal activity. I began to see people commit various unusual types of crimes. I watched kids drift into various kinds of misdemeanors. But in our household, even the idea of crime was not tolerated. We were dirt poor, living on an old farm in northwest Florida, but my parents allowed no excuse for doing wrong. I heard my acquaintances discuss how they had stolen things that did not belong to them, but none said their parents made them return the stolen items. Perhaps they didn't know about the behavior. I hope this was the case. I say this because I later learned of parents who were aware of their children's criminal behavior but refused to do anything about it. Many failed to see a criminal pattern developing out of petty thievery.

Teenagers who are allowed to continue in petty crime will ultimately move on to bigger, more serious crimes.

During my high school years some kids would go down to the local store and shoplift and take what they wanted. Many stole in order to belong to campus cliques. What a tragedy when we honor those who steal. Those who committed petty crimes did not see a criminal pattern in the making. Some did it just for the fun, for the kick of it. But in reality they were drifting into a world of crime without realizing it. To many, stealing was far less strenuous than working to buy what they wanted. It was easier to go into a store and steal a candy bar than work and collect soda bottles to sell for money. My parents had taught us to never steal, but to work for what we wanted. We used to collect soda bottles and take the nickel or dime paid to us to purchase our candy bars. We learned about integrity and honesty and took satisfaction in doing what was right. Unfortunately, many in the Black race have failed to see the eternal value in integrity and honesty. Taking what does not belong to them is just a way of life. The tragedy of this thinking is that it destroys one's image.

Dreams Busted by Crime

I remember a high school acquaintance named Bobby, who got caught up in crime. Bobby had never wanted to be a criminal. Interestingly enough, I had spoken with him, and he had big dreams, big ambitions that included college.

Once I asked him, "Bobby, what is it that you want to do with your life when you grow up?" I can still hear his reply. "Chuck, I want to be a professional football player someday." He had the talent to play pro ball. Here was a young man with great potential, but when no opportunity presented itself when he needed it most he chose a life of crime. Needless to say, Bobby never reached his potential in life and his dreams went unfulfilled. Because he couldn't wait for legitimate means to achieve his dreams, he threw them all away. Unfortunately, he needed others to help him find an identity that only God could provide. He had not started out stealing small things the way others did. After growing up in a neighborhood where crime was a way of life, he too eventually committed crimes ranging from petty theft to armed robbery.

Many young blacks are still making this mistake today.

Sometimes while I watch a football game, it's as though I can still hear Bobby say, "One day I'm going into the National Football League and become a star running back." He was not simply fantasizing about a pro ball career. Seeing him play, it was easy to believe he would someday make it. But as with all of us, there were several key factors missing-- the opportunity and the determination to succeed in a world where many take the easy way out. Perhaps he had neither when he needed it most. But I am convinced he could have made it had he stuck it out to the end, and held on to his dream.

Crime is a huge dream-buster for many Blacks. I'm certain many Blacks have had big dreams, but the daily grind of the ghetto does nothing to help them overcome the temptations they face. This is not to say that they have no alternative, but the opportunity to escape may not be available when they need it most. As a result, a person's dream may become a nightmare. Bobby was a black person with a dream. And I am convinced that had he had a relationship with Jesus Christ, Bobby's life would've been different.

There is much to be gleaned from this man's story. Many young Blacks have the potential to make a significant impact upon the society. Some years ago, I learned that Bobby became a crime statistic when another young black male decided to put a weapon to his head and kill him. Obviously, it is too late for Bobby, but it's not too late to encourage every young person that there is a God who can help them find their identity. Too many Blacks escape into alcohol and drugs while their dreams go unfulfilled. The lesson here is that illicit behavior cannot fulfill our purpose and give us identity, because only God can do that.

In fact I am appalled at how unaffected we are as a culture when we hear about crime. My wife and I were listening to the evening news the other day, and there was a story about a rapist who had attacked several females. The story that followed was about robbery. As the news continued, I realized how jaded we've become to the devastation around us, to the pain of those affected by crime.

Personally, I believe that those who commit crimes have no idea of who they were meant to be. As a result, they have to harm others to feel significant.

I say this because of experience gained some years ago from accompanying my college criminology professor to a prison for a research project. While interviewing male prisoners as part of the research, I asked this question: "What led you to committing your crimes?" In almost every case, the problem was traceable to poor self-esteem. They turned to crime as a means to become someone important, even famous, though for the wrong reasons. But in the end, their behavior would take them further away from the significance they yearned for. How strange. The truth is that criminals hurt others to gain self-importance and recognition.

During my study inside that prison, I learned that people do strange things for all the wrong reasons, believing their behavior logical. Within black communities drug and alcohol abuse is pervasive. Although the sale of alcohol to adults is not illegal, it may well contribute to the undesirable behavior of those that abuse it. It may well lead to other criminal activities. Any illicit means of making money is unacceptable to God. Alcohol and drugs are slow killers of both bodies and dreams within the black community.

In our effort to understand Blacks and the silent killers that deceive them, we only have to look at skid row, jails, and the cemetery to recognize the devastation they cause.

No matter how we see the problems of contemporary Blacks, we are often the culprit responsible for much of our own predicament. The majority of drugs are sold by black males between the ages of fifteen and forty-five.

Do those who push it on the street care about the consequences? I seriously doubt it. Clearly, both buyers and sellers suffer from identity problems. Drug dealers are not unintelligent people. Managing the drug operations and avoiding apprehension require planning and intelligence. But their business has a negative impact on society. It laces the veins of young and old, giving false hope to those in search of identity. Drug dealing is a multi-billion dollar business. Of course those who push the nickel and dime stuff don't get rich, but they do enjoy success in their own way. In a visit into many of the ghettos, drug-selling operations occur in broad daylight. Drug dealers used to try to cover their operations, but that is no longer the case. Though police make every effort to rid the communities of drug sellers, most manage to move on just before they get caught. There are not enough law enforcement officers available to stay on top of the problem. America's unguarded borders allow large volumes of drugs into our country. Once the poison has crossed the coasts, it spreads rapidly into the inner cities. I have always wondered why Blacks are so often victimized. By this I mean black households cannot afford to lose any of their incomes without causing other problems for their families. Yet, it is in the black communities where drug dealing seems to be so profitable and prominent; there is no shortage of buyers. One would think we would be wiser than to fall prey to yet another deviant behavior that shortens or ruins lives. Death eventually claims everyone, but drug-related deaths and crimes affect black neighborhoods more than others.

Drug users fall into one of two categories: Those who have money and use drugs to escape boredom, and poor Blacks who barely scrape by and use drugs to escape the depressive effects of poverty. The rich can eventually go into rehabilitation centers for treatment, but poor addicts have no way to pay for treatment. Often, they are killed in drug-related crimes or die from diseases like AIDS.

In both groups, drugs have a negative effect, but in poor areas the effect is usually lasting and breeds additional criminal behavior, eventually becoming a vicious cycle. The presence of drugs tends to breed other crimes and vice versa. Year after year the media reports the tally of drug-related deaths. But so far this has not discouraged those looking for their identity in the drug culture. From the crime statistics and my point of view, the negative effects of drug use have only increased over the years. What kind of effects? Let me share my experience in talking with people I have known who discovered themselves caught in the vicious web of drug addiction. The names have been changed to protect their identity.

In 1974 during my internship as a student at Florida State University I was assigned to work with a young man by the name of John. John was a twenty-six-year-old black male inmate incarcerated in a northwest Florida Prison. He was convicted for selling cocaine in the inner city of his hometown. I was assigned to interview and discuss his life in prison. In the spring of 1974, we met to discuss how he ended up in prison. His life started going bad around the age of fifteen. He had come from a middle class black family and attended school in the Tallahassee, Florida School system. During high school he was on the basketball and football team along with several other Blacks. Over time they began to smoke marijuana. Before long he hung out with these companions during school and on the weekends. At times, they would cut class together and go to various sites to do drugs. At that point he began to smoke frequently and even to use cocaine on occasion, which is the point where his life took a turn for the worse. Due to failing grades, he had to repeat his junior year, lost his starting position, and was eventually kicked off the football and basketball teams.

He saw that he was slipping into a life of crime but felt helpless to do anything about it. At one of our sessions, I remember asking him, "What was the worst mistake you made?" He replied, "My worst mistake was going along with classmates to do things I knew were wrong." This prompted another question, "Why did you go along with them if you knew they would lead you astray?" He said, "They offered me something I hadn't felt before." I said, "And what was that?" He replied, "The chance to belong and be accepted without expecting anything from me."

I asked if he still felt they expected nothing from him. He replied, "Since those days I have come a long way and understand that no one does anything without expecting something in return." I shared with John that Jesus always does things for us without expecting anything in return. In I John 4:19, it says He loves us without waiting for us to love him first.

Six months later he was trained to use a weapon and in time found himself not only using drugs but selling on the streets. A couple of years later he was arrested for carrying an illegal weapon and selling cocaine to an undercover police officer. John was just one of many fooled into the criminal subculture believing it would cost them nothing. Drug dealers are always looking for young Blacks, and especially males with no self-worth who seek to belong.

As I think back on that session with John, I can still see his face as he explained how he began a life of petty crime and was later convicted of using and selling drugs. Eventually he was into big time crimes that landed him in prison for ten years. When he first met his friends, he had no intention of using and selling drugs because he had been raised with different values. The group at first demanded nothing, but later on, drew him deeper into the web of manipulation, deception and theft, one with a costly price

Some thirty years later after working with John, I became a pastor and, met a young lady name Kim. She asked me if I could talk to her about a drug problem. I met with her and determined that she needed professional counseling. I contacted a drug and alcohol treatment center to seek professional help for her. At our first session I asked how she got involved in drug and alcohol abuse. She explained that she had lived drug and alcohol free prior to attending college. Once in college, she attended sorority parties where she drank and eventually smoked marijuana. Her grades began to decline, and she failed a couple of her classes. For three years she had been using drugs and drinking alcohol heavily. I asked her, "What is it that these substances do for you?" She answered, "They let me escape from the things I don't like to deal with."

Many people use drugs and alcohol as a means of escape. When she first became involved, she had no intention of getting hooked. But on dates, guys would purchase her drinks because she was attractive. One day, she had been asked to sell some cocaine and did, but refused to do it again. Although the money was good, she did not want to become involved in the drug subculture.

However, she continued to be influenced by other users. Within a year she needed substances to control her everyday life. It was at this time that someone told her to seek counseling help. I asked her, "What made you start using?" She pondered the question momentarily and answered, "The need to fit in."

Not long after getting to know Kim and working with her problem, I came across another person suffering from the ill effects of drugs. It was a cold rainy day as I traveled home from work. A young black lady was trying to hitch a ride across the Woodrow Wilson Bridge after her car broke down on the way home.

I probably would not have stopped had the weather been better, but on this particular occasion I did. She asked if I had any marijuana and I said, "No, I don't do drugs." She then offered me her body if I would stop and buy alcohol and take her somewhere to drink it. I almost put her out of the truck, but the Lord wouldn't allow it. Instead I told her,

"No, because I belong to the Lord Jesus and I have a wife to whom I am faithful." I told her I would drop her off at the next exit. When I let her out of my truck, I stopped to pray with her, and when I finished praying, she said, "Thank you sir. No one has ever done what you just did for me." She said, "Years ago I got turned on to drugs and alcohol by my boyfriend and have regretted it ever since, because it is a demon that gradually but surely, kills." I prayed with Cherie before leaving her and told her to check herself into one of the several twelve steps drug and alcohol abuse centers in the Washington Metro area to get help to get clean.

Those who have never been involved with substance abuse can't identify with those who would sell their bodies for a six pack of beer, or bottle of liquor. Yet, I am a witness that it happens. Kim, Cherie and John were young Blacks, and though they had not grown up in the ghetto, their lives had become entangled with those who used or sold drugs, and abused alcohol. They became victims of their own lusts. What started out as a search for significance landed them in worse predicaments.

Whenever we discuss drug and alcohol, we need to consider the wide availability of illegal substances. Inner cities and suburbs, too, have many hidden places that sell them. People can manufacture certain drugs in the privacy of their own homes. And unless authorities have credible evidence to obtain search warrants, they are untouchable. The drug problem is so vast that an easy answer seems unlikely.

One of the primary problems facing those charged with eradicating drug marketing is that users tend to protect their suppliers. In inner city ghettos, individuals actually look up to the very people who poison their children and families. As long as Blacks allow sales in their neighborhoods, the problem will not end. Until Blacks decide they are fed up and begin to report illegal activities in their neighborhoods, nothing will change.

There are numerous success stories of Blacks who decided to work with authorities to clean up their neighborhoods. When we take the responsibility to stop illegal activity, there will be a significant reduction in drug trafficking. In fact, research shows that the success of enforcement efforts depends on local involvement.

Fear is another factor that prevents Blacks from getting involved. Clearly, the best and only way to take back a community from drug lords is to walk away from apathy and report all questionable activity.

Alcohol is just as big a problem in our communities today as the drug problem. I am amazed at the vast number of liquor stores that exist in inner city black neighborhoods. Whenever liquor stores move into an area, other crimes escalate as well. In areas where alcohol is sold, people are more interested in satisfying their thirsty appetites than thinking about the will of God for their lives.

One day I counted five liquor stores within a two blocks radius. You might not consider this to be a big deal, but the fact is, it has a tremendous impact upon the economic identity of the surrounding area. Think of it this way: how many liquor stores have you seen in affluent suburb areas? I would be inclined to state not many, because the affluent do not want these businesses located so close to their homes because they perceive they will negatively impact property values.

Research confirms the negative long-term effects of such establishments. Their presence attracts violence and other kinds of crime. They give Blacks a false sense of hope that alcohol will address problems, when in reality it offers only temporary pain relief. Oftentimes it provides companions for those who abuse alcohol; misery loves company. There is not one shred of evidence that liquor stores are spiritually good for the local economy.

What can Blacks do to take back their communities from these influences? For one thing, we must stop tolerating destructive influences. Because we live in the suburbs we are often apathetic about what happens in the inner cities. We believe it's their problem and not our own. We believe as long as the criminal activities remain within the inner cities, we have nothing to worry about. This thinking has polarized the inner cities and made them havens for drug dealers to push their products to the poor and disenfranchised. Truly the long term effect of apathy is far worse than if we support efforts to eradicate the problems. We need to get involved in any way we can to send a message to those who prey on the poor.

Perhaps we overlook the fact that area residents are actually victims. When drug abusers get a paycheck they search for escape into a world of false hope, searching for a reason to live. In their search for someone to love them and a place to belong they become easy prey to drug distributors.

When a race is unaware of its value to God, it is unusually vulnerable. There are costly consequences for the entire Black race when its members decide to use illicit means to establish their identity. One of the most obvious results is overcrowding in the prison system.

New prisons are constantly being built to deal with increasing levels of crime. All over the country black men are being arrested, convicted and sentenced to correctional facilities, removing them from free society and leaving their families destitute. The inmate population of every prison consists largely of black males, and these prisons are becoming more overcrowded each day.

Unless something is done to reverse the increasing number of black men being incarcerated the Black race will continue to suffer more than any other nationality. Overcrowded prisons increase the probability that inmates will become hardened criminals. If they continue to be released into the same crime-ridden neighborhoods, there is little chance they will reform. While prisons do have some effective treatment programs for inmates, prison life presents many challenges. Hatred and interracial violence trouble most prisons, to say nothing of the emotional and psychological injury inflicted by other inmates. And for every overcrowded prison, there are countless children who suffer. A vicious cycle begins when stronger inmates subjugate those weaker than themselves. Many inmates will leave with diseases and scars as well as prison records that will always haunt them. Finding employment to support a family will always be an ordeal. Many return to prison within a year of being released, feeling they have few options other than crime. So, a bouncing ball effect begins to occur.

The overcrowded prisons produce another dilemma for black communities. Each time a male is incarcerated there are fewer potential husbands for our daughters and sisters. Once caught up into the prison systems, black males will struggle to find jobs to support families.

Incarceration causes a hardship on those that have been victimized as well as the families and relatives of offenders. Offenders forfeit their roles as heads of their families, leaving many black women to support the family alone. Women married to inmates often feel betrayed and deserted. They may have married this individual thinking he would be the head of the household and breadwinner, only to discover he has lived a double life—a secret life his wife knew nothing about.

I knew one woman who had married her childhood sweetheart after graduating from high school, believing she knew him and that together they would build a family with solid Christian values. They had known each other since they were six years old and attended high school together. The young woman worked at the telephone company, while her husband was employed at a grocery store, a fairly good paying job for a high school graduate and a black male employed in the South. They had one child and had been married for eight years when things began to go wrong.

One morning she woke when police knocked at her door; they had arrested her husband for trafficking in narcotics. She could not believe this because her husband was supposed to have been working at his job. Confused she obtained a lawyer and went to the jail to seek release for her husband. In less than an hour she learned that her husband had been living a double life. When he was not at work, he sold narcotics that netted him a felony conviction and a prison sentence. The family was soon separated and the wife was terribly distraught.

The wife now had to become the head of the household and she and the child suddenly wore a new label—offender's family. Children are affected by the psychological pressures of having their fathers, or in some cases, their mothers in prison. Each time a black man is imprisoned he leaves emotional, financial and psychological scars on his family. Everyone is affected when black men look for their identity through crime.

Once incarcerated, many find reinforcement for their criminal activity. According to statistics, **a large percentage** of black men who enter the court system are sentenced to prison, while the percentages are much lower for other races. Many Blacks believe that unless steps are implemented to balance the "scales of justice", black males will forever have high incarceration numbers. They argue that the discriminatory practices of the court system are the reason the prison system houses more black men than any other race.

In fact, research shows that because black men do not have money to hire the best attorneys, they are more likely to be incarcerated. Evidence shows that the quality of legal representation in large part determines the offender's outcome. And since Blacks are rarely able to afford good private attorneys and must depend on court-appointed public defenders, the probability of conviction is higher. While there is definitely some merit to the argument, others would argue that black men are much more likely to offend. Regardless of which theory one subscribes to, black men have a greater chance of spending time in prison than other nationalities.

Not only are black men more likely to be convicted and imprisoned, but they are also more likely to end up on death row. There are those who believe this is due to the inequity of the justice system. But whatever the reason, the black race loses too many of its men to the criminal subculture.

Prison is a detention facility built to contain and rehabilitate convicted offenders. What is rehabilitation? It is the process of transforming an individual's deviant bent into behavior that is socially acceptable. We all agree that rehabilitation is necessary, but the most effective means are still under discussion. Since Blacks make up most of the prison population, they are the ones most often in treatment centers. Besides that, many black men who enter the treatment process do not believe it will really help. Once inside prison walls, they began to form their own social system to cope.

I prefer to use the term "criminal treatment" with regard to rehabilitation. Its goal is to restore inmates to mainstream society. In order to understand the impact prison life has on the identity of the black people, we need to understand how the black prisoner sees himself. Few outsiders are aware of what really takes place inside prison walls. In fact, there are various factors that affect the success of treatment efforts. Each prison handles the rehab process differently. Some prisons are humane while others allow more psychological frustration and deprivation. While prison life does not have an identical impact on prisoners, they all experience a significant impact on their identity. Each must deal with living within a closed society and under very strict disciplinary codes as well as a stigma that will follow them through life.

During my study of criminology at Florida State University, I learned much about the effects of incarceration on prisoners. The reason being is because I was privileged to assist my college professor who was writing a book on prison inmates. Once a person is sentenced, he or she must learn to survive within an entirely different social system. Prisoners resort to cliques and subgroups to survive incarceration. Such groups afford inmates a sense of security and protection. For most blacks, incarceration creates a feeling of fear and worry over reprisals.

During this time I interviewed area inmates. All agreed that life inside of the walls was a shocking experience they would like to forget. Most willingly discussed the sexual and mental deprivation they each learned to cope with within their own way.

Inmates in prison must learn to live with the probability of being raped and even killed. They must struggle to maintain their heterosexuality in a homosexual environment. While incarcerated, many refuse to get caught up in homosexuality and still survive. However, many do not and become victims of rape. Many incarcerated Blacks enter prison heterosexual but leave as homosexuals as a result of the harsh prison social system.

Co-existing in a world of homosexuality and lesbianism, inmates suffer along with loved ones outside the prison system. Once involved in deviant sexual behavior, too many Blacks permanently lose their identity.

Violence is another factor inmates must face. Inside the prison walls, anything goes so long as the individual gets his way. A code of ethics is set up, and the inmate must learn to adhere to it if he plans to survive his sentence. Those who do not abide by the codes are excommunicated and run the risk of being killed or severely hurt. There is tremendous pressure placed upon all inmates to conform or suffer the consequences. Excommunication serves as a social screening process that eliminates those inmates who become snitches. Caught in a world of "conform or suffer," inmates surrender many of their personal values and end up with no identity at all. They look out for those within their social groups, and endanger those outside.

Although the total impact of prison life on inmates cannot be completely measured, the probability of inmates suffering severe emotional damage is very high. In other words, once the offender is convicted and imprisoned, there is a very high probability that he will not be the same person at his release. Social pressures and fears of injury or death most likely will cause an inmate to leave prison a more hardened person than he entered. Some research evidence suggests that those inmates who get saved and remain in a close relationship with Christ are more likely to leave prison more socially well-adjusted, and with a higher success rate of rehabilitation. Thus, they are less likely to repeat.

On the other hand, those not transformed by Christ are more likely to become inmates again. In any case, their self-image is severely damaged in prison. Re-entering society will be both difficult and costly. And most importantly, the cost of restoring their self esteem will be almost impossible to evaluate.

EIGHT

Blacks in Pursuit of an Education

Education is what equips us to survive our cultural settings. In the past, Blacks found themselves in slavery, denied an education. As mentioned before, they were not allowed to read and write. Slave owners knew that if slaves could read and write, they would revolt, no longer powerless against their owners. Even though others helped Blacks become educated, the South used every means to prevent them from ever getting an education.

Slave ownership was a very profitable enterprise in the South. Blacks provided cheap or free labor, while white owners profited.

Blacks brought much knowledge to this country even during slavery, but were rarely given credit. And while they had a wealth of talents and skills, they were for the most part unrecognized. If they were recognized, their talents were used without any acknowledgment. As long as education was kept from the slaves they would continue to be dependent on their owners.

Slave owners refused to educate their slaves, hindering them from making personal choices. Our black ancestors did not come to America ignorant or without talents and skills, but they were forced into slavery and denied the opportunity to retain their self awareness. During this era, they lost much of their African heritage.

Notwithstanding the fact they lost much of their African heritage, even during slavery, our ancestors wanted to learn. Historical records prove many black slaves would wait until their masters slept and then learn to read and write by moonlight or lantern light. Some slaves had more education than others. Along with the early abolitionists who would invest their resources and risk their lives, Blacks with some education would help others learn. Before long many black slaves had learned to read and write to some degree, and it cost some of them their lives. That privilege belonged only to plantation owners.

The death of some slaves did not stop others from pursuing a basic education. The determination of those ancestors paved the way for the early abolitionists to take education underground. Soon slaves began to understand that although they were forced to work on plantations, they could learn and begin to take control of their destiny.

When the slavery era ended, Blacks emerged, many well educated. The very thing wealthy Southern plantation owners feared most had come to pass. Many Blacks left the South and went north to get good jobs in factories. In the industrialized North, Blacks had options and were able to contribute to production output. Certainly caring for plantations was not the life God intended for them and they were no longer content to remain on those plantations. Education allowed them to better themselves and their families. While slavery denied them equality and basic human rights, the slave owner's tight control kept them dependent. The determination of our black ancestors to get at least some education led to a new life for every black person, benefiting us even today.

Education has always meant sacrifice and frustration for Blacks. Since the end of slavery black people have been given better opportunities to pursue a good education, but this does not mean there are not still racial barriers that hinder them. Recent Supreme Court hearings involved cases challenging the constitutionality of laws passed years ago to guarantee educational justice for all. These laws would undo the incredible progress made to secure equal educational opportunities. So, although today's Blacks have many more opportunities, the ghosts of yesteryear's racial barriers still haunt Blacks in America.

Teachers and administrators are by law expected to help everyone obtain a quality education. The case of Brown vs. Board of Education sought to correct decades of evil practices. However, the passage of a law did not necessarily correct internal discrimination practices within the classroom. During my college internship, I was amazed at the different practices the school system used to implement classroom discipline. Many of those practices were not fair and sowed resentment in black students who were punished for the very same minor infractions that other races were not. I would interview many of the black students to get their opinion on the conditions in that school system and many saw the inconsistencies practiced within the school. Black students would often complain to the administrators, but because of certain stereotypes, little or no action was taken.

When I left that internship, I knew that as long as black students continued to perceive of administrators and teachers as insensitive, biased, and prejudiced, internal conditions would not improve. Black students often complained that administrators did not understand the Black race. There were cultural differences that did not make it easy for administrators or students. Administrators had not been properly trained in cultural diversity. Most felt black students were undisciplined and troublemakers. In many cases, administrators and teachers had valid arguments. It was clear some black students came to school to disrupt, rather than to learn.

Following the slave era, northern schools seemed to have fewer problems integrating the classrooms than the southern states, while in the South, Blacks had greater difficulty getting an equal education. The southern court system was used to defend the oppression that suppressed the black education movement. Southern Black students who did not cooperate with the status quo were expelled at alarming rates, while northern school systems were ignored because the North was a liberal place, and the South a racist place.

Until investigations were launched, no reports surfaced about northern discrimination problems. Why was this so? Well, during slavery the North had helped Blacks out of slavery. So obviously everyone assumed that black people were seen equal in the North. No one concerned themselves when black students complained. Black parents felt that their children were blessed to be out of the racially prejudiced South, and white parents didn't care one way or the other. Before long, it became apparent that although segregation was not as widespread in northern schools as in southern schools, it was a problem.

Hostility against Blacks suddenly began to rise in the northern states. Northerners were angry when the country uncovered their secret discrimination practices. Soon busing was implemented to bring racial balance within the segregated schools. Busing was a shocking revelation among the so-called liberal, integrated northern states. Although sporadic acts of discrimination had always been a problem in liberal schools, these had largely gone on unacknowledged. Once forced to cooperate, the northern states gained much media attention. Busing became the means to racial balance there as well.

In general, Americans believed that northern schools accepted integration. They were wrong. Instead, the North merely gave the appearance that they did. Compared to the hatred and racism so prevalent in the South, school systems in the North did not have the same types of educational barriers, probably because most Blacks settled in southern states during that time. One might conclude that northern schools were far better than those in the South. However, these schools were not without faults of their own. Whereas integration became more tolerated in the North, both used segregation practices that hindered Blacks from educational equality.

Busing became known as the practice of transporting students from one neighborhood school to another. In essence busing was a court's plan enacted to equalize the ratio of black and white students. It resulted in reassessment of school system values countrywide. By relocating students to other neighborhood schools, the courts hoped to achieve racial balance. And while the idea was certainly valid, many opposed the movement and fought it because they were forced to do something against their will.

While the courts did achieve a certain amount of racial educational balance, private organizations were busy planning a counter move to defeat the purpose of busing. Whites strongly opposed busing because they felt it infringed upon their personal freedom. While the courts realized that busing would cause much controversy, they also knew something had to be done to correct the imbalance.

If the courts had chosen another alternative to busing, the racial balance would have taken much longer to achieve. Freedom was being taught and talked about in the classrooms, but in reality America was only giving lip service. Busing presented the country with an effective and time-sensitive plan to deal with segregation during those years. Blacks did not see themselves as free, because they were being denied an equal opportunity to become educationally incorporated into the culture of their country.

There was an attitude of peaceful coexistence during the busing and integration eras, but without affording opportunities other races had. When the Supreme Court announced that busing was not unconstitutional and could be used to desegregate our schools, hostile feelings grew throughout the country. Both races went through a period of polarization.

States were shocked that the Supreme Court would force people to get together even though one race opposed this law. Citizens felt the court was over-stepping its boundary, denying individual freedom. Chaos was the order of the day. Many white parents took their children out of the public schools and started what became called "home schools." Others started so-called Christian schools. Regardless to how you look at it, busing created a new revolution for American Blacks and Whites. For the entire country, life had taken on a twist that would change the direction of education forever.

We witnessed violence in both the South and the North to prevent school integration. Although more violent resistance occurred in the South, the North also resisted being forced to integrate to Supreme Court standards. For a country that had boasted about equal rights for all, Americans did all they could to prevent it. Whites physically attacked black students bused into their neighborhoods. Violence became severe in many areas. Some folk lost their lives in the struggle for equal education opportunities. At times, violence got so bad that the National Guard was called out to restore order. White and black students were being forced to do something their parents had never done.

Busing was seen as an unnecessary evil in both northern and southern states. Actually, it was not the monster that most people perceived it to be. It was merely a means to remove the educational barrier that had divided America. Incredibly, those early years of busing were totally misunderstood. The courts did this, to inconvenience neither Blacks nor Whites, but to unite a racially-divided nation. The underlying intention of those who drafted the legislation was to eliminate longstanding evils and promise hope for a more peaceful nation. But busing did one more thing for all of us, regardless of our race. For the first time in history, this nation was forced to either put up or shut up.

The American people were forced to disclose their true plans for equal education. What do I mean? The battle of Brown vs. Board of Education did not correct the damage caused by years of segregation. It only put a bandage on a wound that needed healing. While black students were now supposed to have equal rights, this was not what transpired. The whole world watched as our free country refused others the opportunity for educational equality. And perhaps more than anything this was a very good disclosure. Busing gave us insight into our weaknesses not only on the education front, but it reflected a deep-rooted problem that was imbedded in our nation's culture.

As long as the American school systems were segregated, equality was impossible. More than any other factor, busing brought an end of only giving lip service to democracy. Democracy is not just raising and lowering a flag, and extending privileges to one particular race, but to all races equally. Sometimes we have to be exposed to another way of doing something to understand that it does not have to be an evil. Busing was simply another way of changing the world for the better. For the first time, this nation had to face the fact that education needed an overhaul. Blacks were not receiving a quality education; in many cases, black schools were given textbooks and supplies that were already outdated by the time they received them. Thus, their level of achievement was always far behind the state of the art.

Although earlier laws had been passed to prevent this, they were unsuccessful. Education was definitely separate, but by no means was it equal. I for one can attest to the failure of the separate but equal system of education, because I was a victim of that system. Some years ago now, I was attending a school in my small hometown of Caryville, Florida. We did not have a cafeteria, and received all our school materials from the White school system.

Each day we would have to use school textbooks that had been marked in, had pages missing and some were without covers. The tragedy of this was that unless the student stayed focused he could become discouraged. The teacher would teach information that was not even in our textbooks. Yet, we were expected to pass certain state exams. We were required to perform as if we had access to updated information. I recall the times when I felt discouraged because I was struggling to get a good education and did not have the necessary tools to acquire one. Whenever the state test examiners would come to our schools to do testing, I can remember praying that I would score in the higher percentile group. Although I did not understand many of the test questions, I did my very best to use the knowledge I had to make a statement. This was: "I am bright, and I desire to learn." Although it was difficult to concentrate at times, I focused the best I could. I wanted our black school to be seen by others as a success rather than a failure. During those years, I observed the damage of a separate and segregated education institution.

Not only were our textbooks outmoded, but as previously stated, we had no cafeteria. Our principal had to travel five miles each day to pick up food for our school. By the time it was served, it was usually cold and not very palatable. Even the food we received was different. We did not receive the same nutritious meals that were served in the schools in the white community. There were times when the milk that we received was outdated and spoiled. But because our principal had to travel to get the food, we were expected to eat it without complaint and hurry back to class. Lunch was very short, and we understood that this was the way life was going to be.

Education for Blacks has never been easy; there have always been obstacles. I lived one mile from a school for Whites only, but had to walk four miles to the closest black school. It did not matter whether it was raining or cold, I had no choice because Blacks could not attend a white school. There were times when I would arrive at school in wet clothes. Thank God for that old oil-burning heater that furnished heat for our classroom. Had it not been there, I'm sure we would have ended up with pneumonia. Despite the trials and adversities, I managed to learn from circumstances that were often very discouraging and at times even caused me to question my dignity as a black student.

Even after debate, violence, protests and court petitions, the lower courts upheld the decision to bus. After much consideration I was convinced that busing offered a glorious opportunity to improve education for all students. Despite many reports portraying busing as a violation of constitutional and God-given rights, it provided the only realistic approach to the problem. If the courts had made the decision to continue the separate but equal fallacy, this would have led to more rioting and hatred than it experienced during that period of time. Blacks had come to that place where they were seeing the educational gap grow wider. Pressure was on black leaders to expose the problem at the congressional level. Congress and the courts recognized that the nation could not continue to ignore the injustice in American education. Education was about to undergo a change that would not harm other races, but would guarantee that Blacks be given the opportunity to learn and use their minds. Being denied equal opportunity in the education sector meant that Blacks would not have the necessary skills and academic knowledge to help promote their American heritage. The courts realized that to continue denying Blacks the opportunity to learn meant the country was endorsing ignorance. Where ignorance is allowed to breed, people become supporters of alternatives to reach their goals. Problems like racism thrive when people refuse to unite jointly and strive for advancement.

NINE

The Education Dilemma

For over 350 years this nation has worked to improve the quality of education. Our school systems have been modified and changed to reflect the changing world. Blacks have made great strides in education. Yet, in one sense, we have not managed to change the minds of many Blacks. This failure may represent the attitudes of our society as a whole, unable to keep up with a crisis of constant change. We have trusted the institution of education, depending on it to produce human beings who would make great spiritual, intellectual, and social contributions to our society. And while Blacks have made remarkable progress in education they still lag behind other nationalities in many respects.

As a society, we possess twenty-first century technology that zooms far ahead of practice. The result is a negative impact that has often gone unrecognized. There are those who argue even today, that the social, political and economic condition of a culture is largely determined by their educational strides. And if this is true, then as a society we have failed to learn well from the slave era. Formal education must produce human beings who have been integrated into the greater American culture.

Though a good education is essential, it alone cannot impact the culture unless the goal is freedom for everyone. We are one of the most sophisticated nations in the world, and yet today we still talk about leaving no child behind in school. While this is a step in the right direction, it will not bring about real and progressive changes if it is just an empty phrase. Political practices must change to bring about true educational progress within the Black race. Along with educational freedom there must be the desire to implement sincere changes and not just tout empty ideas. And while education has focused on modern day technology, a segment of our nation may have been left behind.

Because we did not challenge our entire society to achieve educational excellence, other social problems occurred. The failure to establish a foundational social order has left us with other problems that will be very difficult to combat. For years Americans were apathetic toward the need for educational balance across the board. As a race, Blacks were not expected to achieve excellence, but just get through school. Neither the white nor the black race focused upon the dilemma that would result. The decision to keep separate schools and invest different amounts into education led us to where we are today. Today, we find ourselves confronted with a serious educational dilemma—what do we do with the black young man or woman who was left behind as a young child? Can we erase the damage done by an education system that advocated creating an inferior intellectual race of people? In every direction we are confronted with evidence that we went astray. As a result, we have humans who have not learned to cope with life and the technological innovations of our day. Many are just beginning to assimilate into the mainstream of higher learning.

Our culture has become technically advanced over the last thirty years, and many problems have been addressed through education, but that has not solved all our problems. Today, science can launch someone into space. Homes are loaded with electronic gadgets. Almost everyone has learned to drive an automobile. Yet, we cannot escape the truth that these things have not been able to eliminate the disparity that still plagues this country. We have become smarter but we have more problems. Along with other educated societies we have succeeded in developing and creating innovations we use to perpetuate inhumane acts on each other. Weapons of mass destruction and guns are examples of such developments.

Education has been around much longer than modern technology. But only recently has there been a phenomenal growth in the number and percentage of Blacks who receive higher education. There should be little doubt that education can make a difference in the progress made by any race of people. What is not so clear is the way a society can measure the overall quality. A true indicator of progress is the higher number of Blacks now getting a quality education paired with the increasing number of those in high paying jobs. Additionally, there are Blacks living in two income families today, whose numbers are also higher than ever before.

The Road to Educational Redemption

Though Blacks have made much progress toward educational equality, that edge will be lost if we are not careful. Not because of a loss of liberty, but because Blacks themselves often fail to understand the cost of freedom. Education is not something that should be taken lightly. It offers opportunities to learn and exercise our minds, opening doors to the future. Indeed, a mind is a terrible thing to waste. Yet, we live in a day when many have lost sight of this concept. If we do not hold fast to these values many precious resources will be lost, wasted.

Scripture challenges us to build on the solid foundation of God's Word and seek to emulate the character qualities of Christ. Imperfect human beings should not be our role models, but rather Christ himself, our model of righteousness. We cannot afford to ignore the message in

Philippians 2:5: *Your attitude should be the same as that of Christ Jesus.* Blacks especially should see the goodness of God in this scripture, because we were so long denied the opportunity to use our minds in the larger American culture. Through the tireless efforts of our ancestors and freedom fighting Caucasian brothers and sisters who helped, we too, can get an education and rise above the past.

Though we yearn for a better quality of life, we seem to have forgotten that it takes dedication and perseverance to overcome its challenges. Life has never been without some degree of struggle and persecution, no matter what our race. But we must not allow racial issues to become a crutch, an excuse for Blacks to do less than their best.

During my high school years, I decided my life would be different. To make that happen, I used those years to prepare for college. In fact, I went to a high school where I ended up being the only black senior in most afternoon classes. I recall days when I wept over racial abuse and name-calling aimed at me. I understood that our world was not a beautiful place and I made up my mind to help make it a beautiful place for others.

I began dreading class because I was alone and had to take abuse from Whites. But I determined that these things would not deter me from my dream. I knew that the best way to overcome racial hatred and ignorance was to obtain a good education and to show the world the love of Christ who cared enough to die for us, regardless of race or nationality.

As I reflect back on the abuse and mistreatment, I thank God for the strength to survive in such a world. I am even more grateful that He did not allow me to hate those who mistreated me. Although my parents were not highly educated by today's standards, they modeled great spiritual wisdom and love, and they refused to settle for less than our best. They did not allow us to hate or abuse others regardless to how others acted toward us. Fighting in school was forbidden. We were told to carry school issues and problems to the principal and teachers to resolve.

During my senior year, I avoided violence like it was a plague. Other Blacks thought I was weak for backing down, but I only wanted to stay out of trouble. I knew my high school principal was prone to expelling black students. In fact, I remember on numerous occasions when I use to think, why are the black student always at fault? Administrators always seemed to rule in favor of the White students and against Blacks. During my last six months of high school, I recall a fight in the bathroom where six white students jumped a black student and he ended up getting expelled along with the others even though he was just defending himself. I felt that ruling was unjust. Nevertheless this was the way life was and we had to deal with it.

Through that incident I learned how to deal with the truth--that justice was meted out according to the color of one's skin. But was this any reason to give up on my dream? No. Jesus Christ was very much alive in my life and I knew He had plans for me. As ironic as it may seem, the love of Christ made me hold onto my dream during those hard times. There were several obstacles that could've deterred me, and at any point I could have walked away from my dream of going to college. Though obstacles can be enormous, if we, like Joseph in the Bible, can hold onto our dreams no matter what, God will work everything out for our good (Romans 8:28).

I needed an education to make a difference in the world, and getting into trouble at school would have hindered that goal, and eventually stalled my dream. Unfortunately, many of our youth do not see the value in pursuing their dreams rather than settling for less, taking the easy way out. With the media appealing to the minds of both young and old, it's no wonder so many get caught up pursuing the wrong values. This is not to imply that those who fall prey to these enticements should blame the world for their decisions. Each of us must set goals for ourselves, and stay focused on achieving them. This is not always easy, but it is certainly doable. When we see the correlation between making wise choices and how that defines our identity, other things fade into the background.

As a black person, education should not be seen as a struggle, but as an opportunity for a better life. Many of today's Blacks see studying as a problem and not a blessing. There is much evidence suggesting that by studying hard to learn, Blacks can overcome low self-esteem.

The feeling of achievement that comes from finishing school and acquiring an advanced degree significantly impact how he sees his value to society. A better education positively affects crime rates in black neighborhoods, and America. No matter how you look at the value of education, those who are educated always fare better than those who are not.

Over two hundred years of slavery did not force our slave ancestors to be violent and lazy in school. Though they had no opportunity to better themselves, they purposed to use every avenue to overcome their handicaps. Today, we have fewer handicaps to hinder us and yet Black students kill each other over romantic attachments and personal turf battles. We use guns to kill our own people. No, Blacks cannot place all the blame on white society for what is going wrong within our culture. Violence has become a household word in the black community. In fact, it seems as though many Blacks have lowered their expectations of each other, which has only increased their tendency to become violent. A large percentage of the black population is apathetic, and this is taking place after years of fighting for equality and peace.

Were our ancestors' efforts in vain? Did Dr. King's legacy of nonviolence and seeing ourselves as significant--die when he died? Have we forgotten the fact that he fought against wrong without becoming a person of violence? Blacks may argue that the pressures of society cause alarming increase in the violence in our school systems and our world today. But I disagree with this theoretical view because there are some Blacks and other races who refrain from such violence. Is there a correlation between how a person understands himself and his choices in life? I believe most sociologists and psychologists would agree that there is.

Since education is a means to change how Blacks see themselves in a world where they feel insignificant, we must make every attempt to help Black children get a quality education. This effort must start with the parents. Some years ago, parents were not able to provide much educational assistance to their children. But in our contemporary world, this has changed. We can no longer afford to allow our children to fend for themselves, but we must learn together with them. It is a fatal mistake to expect teachers to do all the teaching. While this may appear to be easier for parents, in the long run it is disastrous. The failure to check Junior's homework and meet with his teachers regularly can make all the difference in how he sees his role in the world today.

I am well aware of the additional burden this will place on black parents who strive to buy Game-boys and X-box computer games. But could it be that this is where we make fatal mistakes in parenting? Giving gadgets has become another way for parents to avoid our responsibilities for studying and spending quality time, assuring them every chance for an education.

Gadgets do nothing to provide Junior with the skills he will need to function in a society where other races are better educated and most likely will receive better jobs. Do these gadgets increase his self-esteem and self-awareness? No. In fact, they will likely hinder his ability to see himself as being of value to the world around him.

Rather, the violent drama of video games helps Junior to see himself as a gangster in a gangster world. Rather than encouraging video games, we should spend time encouraging our black children to read and build their character with things like crossword puzzles and math games. While this might not go over too well with our children, I am convinced that once they see the added value in self-esteem and pride they will learn to adapt quite well.

A few weeks back, I read an article that said less television is better for all family members. This might seem crazy, but I really do see the wisdom here. When we spend quality time glued to television and video games, our skills tend to decline. I am much aware that some of our video games do challenge the mind, but in what way? Do they improve black children's math skills? Do they help our children read better? This same study pointed out that while Asian children spend less time watching television than any other nationality; they have made the greatest educational strides visible today. This does not happen by coincidence. It happens because Asian parents are teaching and studying with their children because they want them to overcome their handicap in America.

As black people, can we honestly say that we spend extensive quality time strengthening and encouraging our children to become better educated? Have we taught them the value of putting off their immediate desires in order to prepare for a brighter future? In a world where we are hindered without a quality education, every black parent should set higher standards for themselves and their offspring. Research shows that self-esteem is something that is learned and not inherited. What a person becomes is largely attributed to the household environment in which he grows up. This should challenge us as a Black race to move beyond the Jim Crow and Ku Klux Klan mentality and strive to better educate ourselves. Our children need to be taught that the responsibility to get an education belongs to them. No matter what opportunities are available, one has to take advantage of them to succeed.

While racism does play some part in the outcome, it does not bear all the blame for what is largely a lack of responsibility. The price of ignorance is much more expensive. Consider this statement: "If you think the cost of an education is too high, try the cost of remaining ignorant." This is an undeniable truth.

Blacks must realize they are ultimately responsible for themselves, and they must do what it takes to develop their minds and their skills. This is the only way they will see change for the better.

I see mindlessness as a key to why so many black students fail to achieve. What do I mean by this? It is the failure to attach value to striving to learn.

When I was in school I wanted to not just attend school, but to actually learn and internalize the information being taught. When people feel it is meaningless to believe for something better, they lose the will to reach for something better, and settle for mediocrity. This feeling of insignificance leads to an identity crisis. This attitude led slaves to remain in slavery as long as they did. They did not feel they played a significant part in their environment, nor could they make a difference. Because they could not better themselves, they settled for the status quo, their minds rarely ever challenged. As long as food and clothing were provided that was sufficient. The death of a people occurs when they view themselves as insignificant.

Teenage pregnancy and premarital sex are the results of mindlessness. We pay a grave price for allowing mindlessness to exist without taking steps to eliminate it. Indeed, a mind is a terrible thing to waste!

I see great danger in letting black students go through school believing they cannot learn. I myself was the product of a system that did not help me overcome a learning problem with Algebra and advanced math.

During my junior high years, I made all A's in mathematics. However, when I got into the high school Algebra classes, I discovered that I could not grasp required math concepts well. Although I studied hard, my understanding did not improve much. I became overwhelmed and sought help from my teachers in Algebra, but they did not take the time to help me overcome a major handicap. I recall attending school each day telling myself that I was a poor math student and there was no help for me. No matter how easy the Algebra concepts were, I still struggled with the basics. The whole first year of Algebra, I struggled to understand something that made no logical sense to me.

Yet, there were other students in my high school class who did very well. I remember each time we were given an exam or pop quiz I felt panicky and out of place.

The interesting thing was that I had continually asked for help. After trying to explain, my teacher would say, "You just need to study and work the problems more often." My textbook had practice exercises at the end of each section of the math textbook. I understood well the importance of the relative concepts, but I was so slow in grasping them that I would tell the teacher it was okay--I would understand them better when I worked them alone. The sad thing about this was that I was too afraid to tell her that I was lost, and felt like I was drowning in a world where I didn't belong.

Other students would watch while the teacher was trying to help me. Because of their obvious impatience, I refused to hold up the class. Yet, there I was feeling embarrassed and ignorant. In fact, I would go home and go to my small bedroom working diligently to comprehend the concepts of Algebra. Inside of me, I felt it was wrong for the class to be penalized for my poor math skills. Although I did not comprehend the math principles well, I managed to get a C-grade.

My teacher would often grade on the curve and that helped me maintain a C- average. Those years have come and gone, and I still cannot totally comprehend some Algebra equations. I had to take six hours of high school Algebra, and with the teacher's help, I did manage to maintain a required C average. In college, I had to take six hours of algebra, and managed with tutorial assistance from instructors and other students to obtain a B- grade. As I look back, I wonder if I really could have done much better if I had been tutored and challenged to a higher standard of performance. Today I realize that a mistake was made during my early years. I was never expected to perform well in math, so I developed a phobia of Algebra. The very sight of those equations would cause me to break out in a sweat and feel panic. Until this day, I cannot help but wonder what a difference it would have made in my life had I overcome my weakness in mathematics.

My senior year in chemistry proved the importance of Algebra in the grasping of other subjects. My Chemistry instructor recognized early in his class that I did not grasp the concepts of mathematics. As a result, he watched me struggle to maintain a B average in a class that would have been "A" work. I had planned to become a biologist since I excelled in the sciences, at least until I had to use the math concepts to solve difficult formulas. Again I suffered in cold sweat because I had never mastered more complex levels of math. Today, there are math tutors to help struggling black students. While I am sure that there were probably tutors in my day, I never had that kind of help.

The point is that while in school, it pays to understand the material we study. I never missed a day of my Algebra class. Yet, that didn't guarantee that I would master the subject. The failure to correct a deficiency always guarantees future problems.

There is a tendency for some teachers to identify a learning gap or disability in a black student and accept it as a flaw. Nothing could be further from the truth. What I needed was not to be left alone to struggle, but rather a little tutorial help. I could have overcome my math weakness, but because I was from a black school, teachers allowed me to fall between the cracks. They overlooked my deficiency instead of recommending tutorial assistance. My parents were not able to help because they had not mastered mathematics either. In fact, they could not help me at all in Algebra.

Later in life, I discovered that black students are often seen by our culture as unable to learn or master complex learning skills. Perhaps we can all learn something from this incident. Taking a shortcut to learning is really the wrong choice. The ability to successfully master difficult challenges builds a child's self-esteem. When parents and teachers shield a child from mastering challenges, he will never have the satisfaction achievement brings. Encouraging black students to strive to eliminate their weaknesses actually promotes healthy self-identity. Unfortunately for so many black parents, we fail to realize that short cuts to learning will eventually lead to identity crisis.

It is my belief that most teachers, principals and administrators do try to improve classroom conditions. They implement programs that are thought to work best. Yet, these steps have not challenged many black students to strive for excellence.

Just yesterday, I saw a news story about two young black men who had murdered a man and were being sought by the law enforcement officers. Both photos appeared on the screen. As I watched, several other violent crimes made the evening news. These perpetrators were also young and black. I couldn't help but ask myself--whose fault is it that these youth have taken the wrong path? It's easy for us to point fingers at the establishment and the school systems. But, is it really the responsibility of the school system to protect the world from violent children that we as black parents have raised?

Perhaps we have adopted a hands-off policy regarding parenting. There are researchers who argue that classrooms are failing black students. But I disagree. Perhaps we fail the classroom by sending children to school who refuse to learn. We can change the curriculum but will this alone correct the problem? I seriously doubt that it will. It's easy to blame the school system because that takes the responsibility off of us.

While we can continue to do this and blame others for our shortcomings, the problem won't go away.

Is there any hope for black youths who have fallen through the education net? I believe there is hope for those youths who question and search for purpose. Whether we admit it or not, we as a society are living in the middle of an identity crisis. The refusal of Blacks to deal with the problem is not a good solution. Nor is the answer to allow young people to grow up in a world where education is not strongly encouraged, and later expect them to succeed. Success must start early.

When we allow hopelessness to remain unaddressed, we run the risk of losing some very bright minds. These include those who have rejected education, believing life in the fast lane offers a greater promise for success. They feel that education has betrayed them, or is not for them. But education has not betrayed them. Rather, we as a culture have betrayed education by thinking there is no need for change in the current learning systems. In some ways our educational system has failed to keep up with challenges and changing times.

Years ago students went to school and were expected to learn automatically. Today, cultural conditions and changes have demanded that learning systems evolve and look for more answers. For example, in the past students did not have to function under the same level of intense peer pressure to conform. Today, students feel that they are unimportant unless other students accept them. In other words, much of the identity crisis stems from external peer pressure. They do not discern their usefulness apart from peer approval. Many students find themselves coming to school to socialize rather than to learn. For these students, learning takes a backseat to everything else. They perceive that life is successful when others commend and accept them. And when we add the race factor to this scenario, things only get worse.

Blacks have lived in a world where they have not been fully accepted. Many of our classrooms exactly mirror our society at large. There are black parents who do not feel important either. We only have to look into our communities to see how much we are impressed by and strive for symbols of wealth. In many cases, the bigger the house, and more expensive the automobile, the better we feel about ourselves. These are symptoms of an adult identity crisis. With this as the model, many young people pursue that same status through illegal means. They too are in the middle of an identity crisis. To them education has no value. Instead, a gun and gangster friends are more effective in helping them feel important and get what they want.

As the pace of society quickens, so must our educational system adjust to help those who can't keep up. Video games have replaced textbooks. These gadgets occupy those who believe they can't learn. Do you know how much learning it takes to become proficient in playing these games? They are a challenge, yet Blacks, whether youth or adult, seem to easily master them. This should be proof enough that black students can learn. If they can grasp these video games, they can understand an algebraic equation. Parents need to devote more specialized attention to their students. Teachers and administrators are not responsible for Johnnie's attention or lack of it; parents are. Education must be valued as a rare commodity, precious and vitally significant. Too many black parents fail in this area. Some of us view education as a State's requirement and not as a privilege to enhance our learning skills.

So--what can we as a society and a race do to help? We must begin to see education as a vital tool for future survival and self-worth. Education must not be seen as a chore, but as something to treasure and love. It must become the desire that fuels a young mind to spend long hours in devoted concentration and study. I know that this is correct because I have observed how much time grown black men will spend playing a video game, all day long.

Some years ago, I was finishing a basement for a friend and I was able to observe the hours her two adult sons would spend playing video games. Over the course of several weeks, I saw these two young men get out of bed and head directly for the video games. They had not prayed or consumed any time studying and meditating upon the Word of God or doing any meaningful work. I recall thinking *how in the world can grown men spend all day playing video games?* At times, they would be so engrossed that they wouldn't even hear their mother call them. These two young men should have been doing something much more productive. If they could master those video programs, surely they could have mastered skills required to hold jobs. Clearly, those two minds were being wasted, identifying with a video world to feel significant and successful.

They are representative of a much larger problem. To overcome the problem of Black apathy, we must teach our youth how to learn. We must teach them to have a deeper appreciation for learning, vital to their future. Learning for the sake of learning does not address this problem, but when a person is put in control of his own educational success, it becomes motivating. We must motivate each student to take charge of his own future.

No one should be allowed to go through life without being taught how to learn effectively. Each of us should be challenged to learn, and be given an opportunity to develop our strengths and overcome our weaknesses. Each black parent must tell his child he matters and has significance. It all starts with the parents. The home is their first center of educational development. If the home does not motivate a child to learn, the teacher must work twice as hard to teach. After all, the purpose of education is to prepare people for the future. Unfortunately, some black parents take no interest in this process. At the current pace of technological developments, every moment of time spent without purpose is a lost moment. We will never live that moment again. Our school systems are made up of underprivileged black students in all regions of the country. Putting a student in charge of his future will teach him how to learn, but not all students will end up in affluent neighborhoods

Thus, we must motivate black students to learn even in less than perfect conditions, since the environment will not always easily accommodate the learning process.

Many impoverished neighborhoods exist in America. In fact Blacks make up more impoverished neighborhoods than any other nationality. And yet our nation is the leading superpower in the world. We spend billions in defense and there still is no peace. Technologically, our country has arrived, but there is a large segment of our nation not being educationally prepared to master the technology. Black students make up the vast majority of that segment. Our nation's educators, Black parents and students must work together to eliminate the barriers that hinder the impoverished children.

Circumstances are not the only determining factor in their pursuit of success. With all the money being thrown at the problem, most of these hindrances should be gone. But due to inner city school problems and broken families, many

Black students are hindered in their struggle for success. Parents must teach their children the importance of sacrificing for an education. We must use every tool at our disposal to teach our children the value of staying in school and studying hard.

One of the best teaching tools black parents have is the history of a people that refused to lie down and die. If our ancestors had done what so many of our young folks are doing today, black people would not have progressed as far as we have. Every moment needs to be seized as a learning opportunity.

As I mentioned earlier my parents did not have much formal education. They did not have the same educational opportunities I had. They worked long hours on the farms and in the canning factories at early ages. Their parents died young, and other living arrangements prevented them from acquiring a good education. They understood the hardships that persisted when one had no schooling or formal education. My father had developed some business skills from attending a local business school, and he knew much about handling business and making wise investments. He took steps early in life to purchase land to farm to make a living for his family. He seized the opportunity to become educated and learned how to better himself, even in less-than-perfect circumstances. My mother had less formal education, but she became the motivating force behind each of her children. She understood the value of a good education. Her physical disability did not discourage her in life; instead, she became more determined to see us get a good education.

I remember when I entered my junior year of high school that my mother had a long conversation with me. By now my older brother and sister were in a college and doing great.

She began to instill in me the need to go beyond high school to college. Later, I learned the reason she pushed me so hard. She had overheard a conversation I was having with someone else that after graduation I would work the farm, or go to the North for a better paying job. As a great visionary, she taught me the value of becoming the best I could be. She urged me not to settle for less than God's best for my life.

She could not help me with my studies because of her limited education. Regardless, she still had a huge impact upon my life. Because of her strong faith, she believed God's Word would provide guidance to help me make sound educational choices. Subsequently, I was able to perceive His real purpose for me instead of settling for something less. In essence, she saw the value of an education, not simply as a way to make more money, but as the means to better cope with life and be used by God in a complex world. Education made this possible.

One might be led to think that I must have had poor grades since I had not planned to continue with my education at a college. On the contrary, I had a GPA of better than 3.5. So, why wasn't I planning to go on to college? Because I believed my father needed my help to run the farm as he grew older. My mother's response: "Your father and I have lived our lives and did not have the opportunities you do, but you have an open door, so step through that door." At that moment I realized my mother was a woman of great courage and wisdom. And in one sense, she was well-educated, realizing the value of staying in school and pursuing a quality education. I had an excellent high school education, but was in fact uneducated. My mother became my best teacher in my junior year. As a parent, it was up to her to motivate me to do my best.

Furthermore, she was what I would call a visionary, able to see that times were changing and that a lack of education would be a fatal mistake. Instead of just keeping quiet, she sounded the horn and said, "You can do much better than settling for a life of mediocrity." She had a dream for me and was the strong force that pushed me beyond my own short-term goals. Because she placed such high value on education, I too caught hold of the vision. My mother was an educator in her own right.

TEN

Studying to Show Yourself Approved

The most obvious fact about education is that it takes time. Unfortunately, many have not yet realized that without an education we will be at a terrible disadvantage. Young people today fail to understand the importance of delaying gratification until they have paid their dues, after which they will have the means to earn what they want. Our society has become dependant on advanced technology, and it will need people knowledgeable in this field. Those who are unprepared can't expect to compete with those who have acquired what it takes in the job market.

There is a direct correlation between income and marital stress. As long as many black students fail to recognize the importance of education, divorce rates within the Black race will continue to rise. Education can do much to alleviate problems that haunt Blacks. We dare not give up our dreams simply because we refuse to study hard to accomplish our goals.

A change of attitude would do much to improve lives in our black communities. The better educated a people is, the better prepared it is to deal with life. The Word of God tells us to "study to show thyself approved unto God, a workman that needs not to be ashamed, rightly dividing the word of truth" (II Timothy 2:15). What has happened to the identity of many of our black people today?

While scripture focuses on man's knowledge of God, it does not negate the need to study textbooks that help us to live in the present world. In the same way, it is paramount that black people study to master their crafts or they will not be able to keep pace with mainstream America.

Our ancestors left us a great example to follow. They placed God first in their lives, and used textbooks to learn to read and write. Today, we have computers that write for us. Unless we understand the basics of computer science, we will find ourselves unable to compete in the job market. It is not just skin color that keeps Blacks out of the mainstream job market; it can also be a lack of preparation to master the increased technological demands of a constantly changing modern world.

When microwaves were first invented, many of us thought we could not learn how to use them. I for one felt like a dinosaur living in the modern world. I recall fear in trying to use one. In fact, I was always bothering co-workers when I had to heat up a pastry. Before long, I learned to master microwave technology. I am sure to most folks this was a breeze. But for someone who struggled with new technology, it felt like an enormous accomplishment.

Then came the computer, and I felt totally out of place. It took me some time to learn how to use the personal computer. On a daily basis I would try to master very basic programs because my job depended on it. I admit I was afraid and had much anxiety about failure. I thank God that he placed my White sister Linda Simms and a friend named Valerie Brown in my path. They understood well the automation age, and had patience with me. Because of their kind instruction, I learned to stop fearing computers.

As things are today, more and more jobs are demanding these kinds of skills. Blacks must overcome their fears and boldly grab hold of new skills, which are not beyond their ability to master. Courses aimed at becoming better qualified in technical competencies should be encouraged in black families and communities. Today education is recognized as a universal human right, the doorway that will move a person from being poor to a better middle class life. Unless we focus on helping black students to accept this as truth, many will resort to the easy street life of crime and violence. The truth is that God wants Blacks to have a good education to overcome their challenges.

He is wiser than we are. He knows that unless we equip ourselves to keep up, we will suffer. God wants us to study because a mind that is unchallenged will become a playground for demonic activity. Black males who refuse to study will eventually end up angry, selling drugs and dying young. Too often as a race we blame others for our failures. It is one thing to want to be an astronaut, but it is quite another to study to acquire the necessary skills. Similarly, it is one thing to want to become a surgeon, but it requires dedication and determination.

It takes time to become an astronaut or a surgeon. These are not careers that can be filled without many years of hard work and sacrifice. But this does not mean that it is impossible for Blacks to attain, because there are successful black doctors, lawyers and astronauts. Considering all the challenges Blacks have faced through history, they have done very well.

Sometimes it is hard to visualize the tremendous price paid by our ancestors so that we could obtain a better education. They refused to be denied the chance at fulfilling their dream. Not only this, but they knew that there was a sovereign God working on their behalf. They worked hard to overcome the obstacles before them, and to pursue their dreams. Some of our people want better careers, but will not commit or delay gratification long enough to finish the course. By this, I mean they are not willing to forego those things that keep them from fulfilling their dream. The temptation of sex and other worldly pleasures overrides their love for God and their dreams.

A case in point: I once knew a young man in high school who graduated with me. However, he wanted to enjoy the pleasures of life while he was young. He loved to spend money but refused to work to get it. His motto was, "Why should I expend energy and time working when I can take a shortcut and get satisfaction another way?" This attitude was destined to cause failure. His decision shaped the rest of his life and his downfall. A few years later, he was arrested for selling and trafficking in drugs. He had a very bright mind, but refused to allow it to be challenged because he refused to delay gratification. In other words, he could not wait to enjoy the material things in life, but was determined that he wanted them now. This thinking led him to the drug subculture as a way to quick success.

How sad was this kind of thinking. I had sat next to him in high school for two years. He had spent much time around me and really wanted to advance himself. Later in high school his dream did not change, but his determination and willingness to work and study hard got lost along the way. This is not a rare case. Many young Black males and females face an identical challenge today. They want to be successful, but see no value in going the education route to obtain it. They perceive that waiting for these things is not worth the cost involved. The tragedy is, those who fail to wait do not grasp the exorbitant cost of instant gratification.

What are some of the external causes that contribute to Blacks making bad life choices? Are there societal forces that encourage bad choices? Since where we live affect how we envision our lives, it's imperative that we look beyond our local communities and think globally. Black people must depend upon self-respect and pride to help them strive in a world system where poverty and discrimination exist side by side.

Most Americans are aware that we live in a world order where the color of peoples' skin can get in the way of success. Neighborhoods and communities can contribute toward some of the same social issues we attempt to eradicate. Segregated neighborhoods lead to increased hardships. Thus, Blacks may be forced to live in environments that do not stress education.

Because low income neighborhoods are more prone to attract those who prey on the poor, we must eradicate this element through better educating ourselves. The more we are aware of the opposing forces we are up against, the better we can prepare to overcome them. Education helps us envision alternate means to eliminate the evils thriving in our inner cities.

We do not realize the deadly effect that segregated communities really have on our society. Most of us realize that these communities have problems and have come to accept this as unavoidable.

All too often, our own lack of interest and commitment to help contributes to the hopelessness of our own people in the inner cities. In turn, parents see no need to educate their children well, because they feel that they are surviving. They fail to realize that if they have no dream for their children, then their children will stop dreaming of a brighter future. They will not be motivated regarding how to turn their communities into success stories. Those who visualize model neighborhoods can also help to build them if they can become architects and master builders. The Bible said that Joseph had a dream and he never forgot this dream, even while he lived under the Pharaoh in Egypt. If he had quit dreaming after being sold into captivity, he would have given up and never lived to see his dream become a reality. Joseph refused the sexual advances of a woman because his dream was not temporal, but were based on God's plan for his life.

The media, news and magazines contribute also to the lack of interest in education. Decades ago, parents who stressed the importance of working hard to attain long range goals were aided by outside forces that helped to reinforce the value of a good education. There were news articles, television programs and ads that stressed the bright side of struggling hard to stay in school and succeed. One does not see the same level of external support today.

Things have changed dramatically since those days. The television is loaded with programs that actually plant the idea that quick success is the way to go. In other words, if you really want to pursue another option besides education it can be a glorious trip. In fact, at any time we turn on the television there will be programs and ads that give the young people false hope. They are presented with visions of glamour and wealth enjoyed by celebrities who never obtained a college education. The newspapers discuss sports success stories. They place great emphasis on how stars have been born without benefit of college. Sports magazine give young men and women something to dream about. Sports are placed on a high pedestal and athletes are glorified. In the minds of those unable to divide hype from truth, they become mesmerized by the thought of making quick bucks.

Most of our magazines, even black family magazines are loaded with news articles that glorify the flesh and not the Spirit. Young people learn about life from what they see on the television screens and what they read in the magazines, which are far from realistic. They read glamour magazines and success related stories because they are looking for their identity. They are not that impressed with the preachers and teachers because they don't promise quick success.

Books, magazines, newspaper headlines and other mass media used to place great emphasis on saving for the rainy day. Today, many of these sources are silent. The very same sources that used to emphasize reducing worldly pleasures and sinful habits, speak very little about the dangers of pursuing worldliness. Fifty years ago Blacks did not have the Internet to help encourage them to seek after things of the flesh. Today, this is no longer the case. While parents work and there is no immediate guidance at home, young people visit chat rooms and "my space' venues doing their own thing. We are living in a changed world.

Whereas media sources used to reinforce parental wisdom, they now emphasize ideologies that contradict sound parental teaching. No longer are they told that those who live together outside of marriage should not be admired. Do these young people see these couples as living outside the will of God? Not anymore. These are now role models. Not only this, but they focus on these stars' success stories rather than their evil lifestyles. Glamour and quick success mislead our youth to demand the good life now. Fame and glamour trump morality every time.

Because the dollar is the bottom line, mass media bombards Blacks with buy now-pay later messages, and low-income youngsters become easy targets. They want it all but have no way to make it happen.

The basic argument here is that low-income inner city children, mainly Black, are victims of social pressures that hinder academic achievement. Many do not have parents who help them see through gimmicks and get-rich-quick schemes, and God is not even mentioned as the means to a fulfilled and purposeful life.

Teachers are left to deal with these attitudes. Many black parents blame teachers if their children identify with the quick success crowd, but it is not the teachers' fault. How can we expect them to do something that we are not willing to do?

Parents believe teachers can wave a magic wand and make foolishness disappear. Johnny has been allowed to admire those who drive expensive cars, wear furs and live in luxury. And though parents often watch these programs themselves, they don't take the time to teach their children that get rich schemes are lies of the devil. Many black parents cannot teach their children this because they themselves are sucked in by such gimmicks. As adults we need to stop dreaming foolish dreams and encourage our children to develop a strong work ethic and excellent character.

In the past, parents and society backed up teachers who demanded excellence. Today's teachers teach children who are not prepared to study and learn. Parents must once again begin to prepare children for academic excellence then back up the teachers who teach them. For years, the government has thrown money into social programs or after school programs as the answer to improving the study habits of inner city minority students. But these programs are, for the most part, often ineffective.

Money and programs alone will not address the issues that trouble our youth today. As hard as it is to believe, economic affluence does not guarantee personal fulfillment any more than political freedom guarantees a feeling of usefulness.

The right to vote doesn't guarantee that Blacks will automatically receive equality. Even after one has been granted the right to vote, he may still be viewed as inferior.

No social program will substitute for good parenting and early introduction to Jesus Christ. Life begins to make sense only in context of relationship with Jesus Christ.

Things and programs do not make a person aware of his value. This can only come from knowing God loves us. Over the years child-rearing practices have changed, but not all the changes have been beneficial. In fact, some have largely contributed to the temporal thinking of our young people. Instead of encouraging quick rewards, we need to model and teach our youth that the only things worth having will come by hard work and integrity. This generation will be the leaders of tomorrow.

Abundance was at one time a distant dream, the result of hard work and determination. Because it's easier to succeed today than it was in the past, our children have come to demand it, to expect it early, and without effort.

High school dropout rates have declined over the years. Universal mass education was at one time a mere dream. But today this has drastically changed and most students complete high school. Another half goes on to college and universities. Even far removed from those days on the plantation, Blacks find themselves in an identity crisis. Freedom and opportunity do not automatically eradicate every problem.

So, what can we conclude about the dilemma of education and the identity struggle of Blacks? The process of cognitive growth is what moves us beyond poverty. Education has always played a dominant role in helping any race claim a cultural identity. Blacks continue to make great strides in education, but it is imperative that black parents and teachers stress the importance of working hard and pursuing excellence.

Although government programs claim that no child will be left behind, some schools are war zones, where kids struggle just to get to school. In some schools, police and metal detectors are the order of the day, and learning is secondary to survival.

Although government efforts have improved the learning environment, they cannot alone alleviate the hazards of our classrooms. Black parents must have higher standards and expectations for their children. They must assume the responsibility for discipline and seeing their children get a good education. This will require the nurturing and determination of black parents, theologians, academics, and most importantly, a relationship with Jesus Christ.

ELEVEN

Blacks and the Family Crisis

Few would disagree that the black family is experiencing much unnecessary tragedy. At times, it seems that the news is rarely good in black neighborhoods. Featured stories range from increasing divorce rates to violence within the Black family. Abuse is common among Black families.

While many Black families continue to make great strides, some live a life of drugs, sex, crime and violence. Why do some families escape while others remain trapped?

At one time, such social abnormalities existed only in the inner city and poor urban neighborhoods. In general, Blacks were not considered violent. Teen pregnancies and cohabitation were not accepted as the norm. Homosexuality was not a lifestyle practiced by those who know Jesus Christ. But these are the issues Blacks face today and most will agree these problems alienate and weaken the Black race. The post slavery era had Blacks excited about their new freedom. However, they soon discovered that shackles still bound them. Today, they're bound by a different kind of shackle, yet with the same repercussions.

The black family is undergoing major challenges and changes. One social change that contributed to the change in the black family had its roots in the Women's Movement.

Until recently, the equal rights movement was unheard of. It was that systematic struggle of women to acquire social, political and economic status equivalent to that enjoyed by men. This definition included every female whether or not she wished to be included. Many people saw the movement as a take-off from the Women Suffrage struggle in the early 1900's. Both movements identified injustices against women and launched efforts to free women from second-class citizenship.

The first won women the right to vote. The second involved tactics to overcome male-dominance. The first initiative--voting rights--gave women a foundation from which to accomplish the second.

Both women's movements made strides because the time seemed ripe for change. Women Suffrage paved the way for change regarding women's status in the family. During the early part of the twentieth century the initial strides allowed women to be viewed with more respect. Acquiring the right to vote gave women a reason to challenge other injustices. Furthermore, the right to vote gave women new confidence in themselves apart from dependence on men. And though this era saw progress, it called for change in other areas as well.

The second movement shocked the world. Never had the world witnessed such a collective and powerful effort by women. History may never record the importance of the Equal Rights Movement in applying pressure to implement change in the family structure, but the movement also caused the power structure to examine the injustice that had gone so long uncorrected. Some specific changes included: (1) an increase in women's net income; (2) an increase in the number of women employed; (3) an increase in the social status enjoyed by women; (4) an increase in political recognition given to women and (5) an increase in the status of women within the family, the community and the church. The movement spearheaded a new era of social, political, and economic change that might not have occurred otherwise.

Up until that time, though women were employed, they held jobs that earned very little income. Most of those jobs have since been upgraded on the pay scale. There are additional changes that need to occur to improve the plight of women. Prior to the movement very few women's salaries fell into the upper third income level. Soon laws changed and women began to enter positions paying higher salaries than their husbands'. Of all the changes instrumented by the Women's Movement, perhaps the greatest was the advent of top-level jobs in both the public and private sector. This change offered the opportunity for freedom and self-promotion. Because of their new freedom and the need for personal recognition, the struggle for female equality became a success. This desire for freedom expanded to include black females who found that it offered incredible opportunities for the future.

This change gave black women hope that they could find a niche. Before long, they too had discovered new opportunities for self-expression and individuality. They experienced a significant revision in past roles and tasks. This meant black women could live within society without feeling oppressed by either the society or the home situation. As women's independence grew, they had more decision-making power regarding their finances and their lives. They could enjoy life while feeling that they made a real contribution outside the home. Black women discovered a common but inspiring sense of pride that accompanied their new social status. It afforded them the opportunity to experience inspiration, expectation and dignity that they had only dreamed of.

Ironically, the Women's Movement received strong endorsement from the community, the family and the church. Although none of these venues endorsed the radical views expressed by the movement in general, all three gave verbal consent to the idea of equality. The irony is that the family, the community and the church were now giving approval they had previously withheld. When they agreed it was time for a change, society was forced to examine its own role. People are the interconnecting link that influence significant change in a society. Any social changes in our institutions are indicative of the changing nature of values, goals and philosophies. White women signaled that it was time for a change, and Black women supported this notion.

Soon the family, the church and the community stood up to demand equality for women. This led to the black woman's desire to move away from the traditional homemaker role. She signaled to the world that it was time for her to experience independence. Thus, social progress not only transformed her support role within the black family, but even her intimate relationship with her spouse. Success created unseen confrontational issues for the entire black family. Black families would have to learn to compromise and forget much of the traditional upbringing they had learned in order to weather the changes intact.

The resulting social change demanded that the black family learn to receive strength from each other. Slavery had torn apart the black family's roots. The end of slavery opened the door for restoring the black family structure. The Women's Suffrage Movement tested the solidarity of the black family. Following the success of women in general and black women in particular, the chauvinistic role of the black man was challenged and would have to go, for the black family to survive the changes.

Today's black man must learn to adjust and become less confrontational in order to maintain family unity. The movement opened a new door of freedom, and it had nothing to do with skin color, but with gender, increasing Black family stress. Many black men adjusted to the change, though many did not because it forced them into direct confrontation with women. In many respects, the black woman relishes her freedom, because of the opportunities it affords. On the other hand, she and her family must learn to overcome the social dysfunction that troubles them.

Divorce rates are steadily increasing, as are incidents of spouse abuse. Lately, violence has even found its way into the homes of the church leaders and clergymen.

In one recent news story, a person was violently attacked while riding a metro-bus. Things have really deteriorated when one can't ride a bus without worrying about violence.

One might be led to think of urban inner city communities when considering dysfunction, because until lately most of these problems were unheard of in the suburbs. However, the sociological landscape has drastically changed for black families. Divorce, hatred and self-rejection were not troublesome problems for black families the way they are today.

These problems have a tremendous impact on an already weakened family structure. It's clear that merely escaping slavery did not end problems for Blacks.

The change in today's black family is startling. Even the makeup of the old extended family has undergone change, and today we see an entirely different black family emerge. Whereas once black families were large, they are now small. The extended family is no longer viewed as vital to family unity. Black families used to be made up of parents and at least one grandparent or close relative. Today, this has changed and left the black family without this extended support and value system passed from generation to generation. In today's world, a large black family poses new challenges. The world economy has drastically changed, forcing Blacks to struggle to take care of their families. There are exceptions to this, especially in poor areas of America. Poor Blacks are more likely to have larger families. But overall, the size of the black family will continue to shrink.

The basic need for the family has not significantly changed; it is still the venue that teaches and models values. Although different cultures have different values, customs and traditions, all social groups have similar social functions that only "family" can address. Within the last half century, though society has undergone change, the functions of family have remained constant. In general, the black race continues to depend upon the family for childbearing and rearing, and control of sexual behavior. However, within the last decade, parents have relinquished much of their control. They are having less influence on the behavior of their children, because they spend little time at home. More and more, the values of young Blacks are being influenced by their peers. In fact, the family as once known is still being reorganized to reflect the changing social mores of our contemporary world.

As the role of the traditional family changes, a new set of contemporary values is being imposed on families of all races. Black families in particular are feeling the stress of escalating divorce rates, women rights, and the economic struggle to survive. Some of this impact is a direct result of individual freedom winning over group needs. Spouses can now leave if they become unhappy. Children have external social and government resources to depend on should their family unit be dissolved. The black family is experiencing trauma, but not beyond redemption and restoration.

Selfishness has become the most dominant factor that plagues the stability of the black family as a whole, just as is the case with every other race. The drive to satisfy personal desires takes precedence over the interests of the family. Thus, the family is forced to readjust, often leaving single women to raise families. When this occurs, the family becomes subjected to additional stress.

If black families remain centered around women and children and exclude fathers, other social problems often result. Even middle class black families with two incomes struggle when the wife works many hours outside the home. Black families headed by working females often leave them without the emotional support they need to keep the family together. Then, there are families headed by two parents who are too busy trying to make a name for themselves to see the damage being done within the family. This pursuit of individual dreams and material things threatens the foundation of strong black family units. More importantly, it undermines the identity of family members. Economic success comes with a high cost. And that cost may be family values and identity. Society now endorses individual preferences ahead of group needs. This eventually leads to family breakdown.

If a family member becomes interested in success at all costs, this occurs at the expense of the family unit as a whole. The black family has always understood that its members must compromise their own self-interests for the good of the group. When members elevate the sense of self, the family unit begins to crumble. As a result, it is much more difficult, if not impossible to remain strong and united. This state of flux creates an additional crisis for blacks in search of an identity. Many mothers seek fulfillment and economic independence outside the home, leaving children to fend for themselves. This is the new norm in our world today.

The contemporary success of the black family has come at a price. Prosperity has significantly impacted the social and moral values of the black culture. Many sociology experts question whether the price is too high.

It is not easy to raise black children in a society where autonomy and curiosity take precedence over self-discipline. And although it is not easy, it is still possible. There are black parents who have succeeded in maintaining strong family values and staying a godly course.

Perhaps too much attention has been paid to personal fulfillment and individual interests, while de-emphasizing discipline, hard work, and self-respect. There is a declining interest in family values in our culture as it takes a backseat to earning money. With black family members pursuing the dream of success and neglecting the godly values of our ancestors, the plan has backfired and produced a generation that departed from the most precious gift they'll ever have-- the one King Solomon requested from God-- "the wisdom to know the difference between right and wrong."

Many black educators are left to wonder if they have been given the responsibility for producing new values to those entrusted to their care. Historically, it has been conjectured that the black family structure was ruined during the slave era. Thus, many educators believe black parents are looking to them to restore the old black value system of the past. This idea is unacceptable. The period immediately following the end of slavery saw black families still spiritually thriving with strong family values.

Black historians agree that the black family was damaged by slavery. But research supports the idea of strong family values subsequent to the end of slavery. During the latter half of the 1800's and the first fifty years of the 1900's, the value system of the black family survived intact.

The post slavery years were not marred with high divorce rates and crime. Men and women cooperated to maintain a household with strong family ties and traditional values. Children were taught respect, dignity, hope and obedience. The quick avenue to victory and success was not a part of the early to mid 1900's belief system. The belief that God could address any problem was a chief part of the teaching of most households.

High divorce rates and single parent households did not appear until after the end of slavery. It appears that these changes can largely be attributed to the generation of the 1950's and beyond.

Current problems can be traced to the decline in godly values, moral absolutes and educational ambitions. These values are necessary to build strong family identity. Over the years, these values have continually declined in many black families.

More than a third of all black families live in poverty. Approximately one-fourth of the black population receives public assistance of some kind. Unfortunately, unemployment is the highest per capital in black families. Taken together, education, employment, and low income spell future trouble for black families.

There is a great latent crisis in the black family and community. This has caused many to question: Is the black family failing? Years ago, most blacks tended to ignore those who warned that the black family was heading for spiritual bankruptcy.

With the sexual revolution came an additional test. The number of Blacks seeking divorce underwent a significant increase. Similarly, the number of black children born out of wedlock continued to rise. More black teens became sexually active at younger ages. The higher percentage of sexually active teens meant that AIDS would increase, and it did. No, the black family will not disappear. It will survive in spite of the attacks it is currently experiencing. Just as slavery did not destroy it, neither will the present challenges. However, survival demands that individual desires and personal gratification be delayed for the greater good of others. Too much freedom can be devastating if it is not based on the will and purpose of God.

TWELVE

Blacks' Second Freedom Quest

At the end of slavery, many folks mistakenly believed that since Blacks had received their freedom they were equal with the rest of the world. Indeed, Blacks were told to go out and grab a piece of the good life for themselves. But before that they first had to struggle to define their individual identity; they had no clear understanding of their value. They were given freedom to go and become a part of the American dream, but with few of the necessary tools to succeed.

The sexual revolution led to added pressure on the black family structure. Freedom without clear identity led them into a different kind of slavery.

As black families struggle to discover what they really want out of life, they must be willing to accept the necessary changes and responsibilities that accompany personal freedom. They must be willing to overcome those negative forces that hinder rather than help them to succeed as a healthy family unit.

<u>The Black Female-who is she?</u>

The black female has struggled over the years to become her own woman. During slavery, this was not one of her goals. She was too interested in trying to preserve the family unit. Her goal was focused around surviving the ills of slavery. Slavery robbed her of personal dignity, but the women's movement promised her an opportunity to regain self-esteem.

When she first came to America she was immediately stripped of pride and confidence that gave her a sense of value. Her independent status was revoked, and she was relegated to insignificance. No longer was she considered to be beautiful and the queen of her home. Instead, she was told she was ugly, a baby-making machine, and an ignorant housekeeper or field servant. In her motherland, she had enjoyed some level of rank and family significance. Taken from a country where she had lived free, she found herself in another country far away without status. She became "**the woman without a face.**"

Throughout the slave era, she became the keeper of the plantation house, a field worker, and a ready supply of free labor. As the cook and laborer, she learned to manage her own household, even if it was only a shack. She learned to endure being relegated to mere housekeeper status. As a result, she soon lost her identity as a special person, and accepted her forced identity as a black servant.

Although the black female lost her original role in the family, she never fully relinquished her longing to be an individual with an identity of her own. Even separation and degradation could not destroy her will to succeed and survive. Her goal was to be free once again. And while slavery robbed her of her status and family role, it could not kill the internal drive to hold onto her dignity and personal determination to survive.

She emerged from her past a spiritually stronger woman than before. Instead of lying down to die in self-pity, she took control, doing whatever it took to survive the inhumane conditions of the day. With the power of God, she managed to become productive and successful in the slave environment.

In the spiritual, political, social and financial world, the black female of today has prospered. Her outstanding ability to take a little and build upon it reverts back to her ancestors' ability to co-exist in a small shack, yet hold onto what remained of the black family structure. The black male was often sold to different plantation owners leaving her to keep the rest of the family together. She became the head of her household.

Much of the credit given to modern day black women for developing strength had it roots in slavery. A rich tradition of perseverance and stamina is seen in black women today. They learned from their mothers and grandmothers how to survive and weather the storms. Today's black woman understands it takes courage and strength to guarantee the survival of her family. And while her independence is precious, she has not abdicated her role as a strong tower of support and integrity within the black community.

Today, she is a very active part of the work force, but her passion for maintaining a united family remains strong. When her man walks off and deserts his family, she holds the family together. She has not forsaken her motherly role. It takes love and dogged determination to survive abandonment and isolation. Nothing has really changed over the years. The black woman works both inside and outside of the home. She is a very precious vessel.

Today black men are incarcerated or killed in greater numbers than ever, leaving the black female to fend for her family alone. She loves her children more than life itself. She has learned to depend on herself and God to make it. She may contemplate getting married one day, but quickly acknowledges, "I must depend on no one else to take care of me." This is her way of preparing for desertion.

Unable to rely upon the black male to provide for her, the black female has become more and more independent. Over the years, in many homes she has assumed the role of head of the household, instead of the help meet. Just like other women she was not designed to be the head of the household, but to assume the supporting role. Nevertheless, at some point the significance of what God wanted was lost. Subsequent to the 1960's freedom quest, the black female became stronger and a more independent force in the black family.

With her new sense of freedom, she discovered that family and identity problems increased. In many cases today, the black woman is the primary or single breadwinner in the home. In many respects, she has lost her knight in shining armor, and at times finds herself going head to head with the black male for leadership of the black family. She is more likely than he to have a good-paying job and in many cases she earns more. Further, she is more likely to attend church than the black male. In most cases, she is the spiritual teacher and leader of the family. This has led to increased internal stress. Yet, the Bible explicitly instructs us that as men this is our responsibility. Being placed in the role as spiritual leader will present additional problems for a people already suffering with an identity problem.

Over the past few years, the black female has suffered a significant increase in spouse abuse. This violent behavior is a direct result of the identity crisis occurring within black homes. Her independence and financial self-reliance have left many black males with a terrible sense of inferiority and inadequacy, which leads him to lash out in anger.

As she loses trust in her man, he becomes more resentful toward her. In both genders, this has become a major problem. Family violence has more than multiplied within the last five years. Abuse of black women is both degrading and unacceptable, and there is absolutely no excuse for it. Black female slaves suffered through abuse and rape. It's time all men stand up and protect women, the weaker sex. God does not sanction abuse under any circumstances.

When the evening news highlights increasing instances of spousal abuse, it should alarm us. While the women's suffrage movement relieved certain problems, by no means did it solve the black woman's quest for freedom.

Recent cases of spouse abuse have reminded us just how serious this identity issue really is. Spouse abuse is not a new phenomenon in black communities, but the significant increase should be a wake-up call. Recently, I have read several news stories detailing extremely abusive treatment perpetrated by black males upon black females. In each case, the intense cruelty revealed the depth of violence within many black families. And if the cycle doesn't end, it will cycle from generation to generation, perpetuating the horror of abuse. Black communities cannot afford to ignore the fallout from abuse, but must deal with it head on.

If the abuse cycle doesn't end, women may come to accept the role of victim, feeling they deserve abuse. Boys as well may role-play the abuse they saw at home, and feel they have every right to abuse women.

Psychologists agree that those who grow up in abusive homes are twice as likely to become abusers. On the other hand, where love is demonstrated, families are more likely to handle family conflicts in loving and mature ways. Ephesians 5:28 tells man to love his wife as himself. Love turns away wrath. For too long, black females have suffered abuse and were afraid to report it.

Much of the violence within school systems can be traced back to the home environment. Unless dealt with in a timely manner, black males will learn to use this as an accepted means of control. As they struggle to handle personal and financial problems, they will vent anger toward spouses or significant others. As internal pressures increase within black families, men must learn to deal spiritually with their families in accordance with the instructions of the Bible.

So far, too many churches have failed to rise up and play a larger role in speaking out against the issue of spouse abuse violence. As divorce rates rise and violence increases, the church must take a pro-active role in this struggle. By sitting idly by, the church becomes a party to the destruction of the black family.

For too long, black families also kept quiet about child molestation, and today black adult victims are just beginning to wrestle with the psychological damage done largely because the issue was kept under wraps.

There are some problems that time will not heal, and it is necessary to confront them with therapeutic intervention. When the home becomes a stronghold of tension, instead of a reservoir of love and peace, family members will be affected. Positive reinforcement and encouragement builds good self-esteem, while discouragement and constant criticism destroys a positive identity. Ephesians 6:1 tells us as parents not to provoke our children. Why did God say this? He knows this destroys their self-image. Too many black neighborhoods are a vivid example of this problem, where guns and knives are used to express frustration and anger. It too often ends with a gun or knife used to commit another violent act. This affects us all and is a society problem and not just "**a black thing.**"

Have you ever witnessed a public outburst of a mother's anger toward her child? What were your first thoughts? Whenever I have seen this, I wonder what message this is sending to the child. If violence indeed births violence, the child will deal with frustration using violent means as well. Or maybe you have seen a black female unleash her anger on a husband or a friend? This may occur when emotional issues go untreated, and the pain inside will eventually be expressed for all to see.

All too often, those emotions will be played out in the divorce court. In a quest to be free from abuse, the black female turns to divorce. Left with no alternative, she will use the legal process to liberate her from domestic violence. Not only this, but all too often the court may fail to protect her from an angry black male, and in the end, she will be injured or killed. Though caught up in a struggle to protect herself, she may still question her decision to leave.

In many cases, she will make the decision to remain rather than leave the violent situation. Remaining in an abusive situation will do nothing for her self esteem, but will do much damage if left unaddressed. There are agencies today that can help with spouse abuse and violence. But the decision to leave an abusive spouse or boyfriend can be further complicated if children are involved. This can be another deterrent that keeps her from leaving. The church needs to take a much larger role in discouraging and preventing such abuse through training and counseling programs. Healthy individuals make healthy families and communities.

I am reminded of just how negligent our own Christian resources are in addressing the violence problem. A few months ago, I read a newspaper article that reported that many large churches do not preach against spouse abuse because pastors feel the problem should be worked out internally. Needless to say, I was appalled at this response. God's Word explicitly condemns such behavior, and does not expect it to be dealt with only within the home. The church must expose and deal with these issues. I read about one minister from a large church who had been warned about his abusive behavior, but was not referred for professional treatment or accountability. Before long, this man was found abusing again.

The failure of the church to expose this problem may have hurt the Black race more than anyone knows. I do not mean to infer that the church is at fault for abuse, only that its leaders must speak out about this evil. Apostle Paul wrote the 13th chapter of I Corinthians on the positive effects of pure love. In Ephesians, he points out how a husband should love and deal tenderly with his wife, not with violence and abuse. The time has arrived for churches to seriously address this issue.

The black female's struggle and search to discover her own individual identity can be confusing. Her struggle to be free is still not resolved in many areas of her life. Many black women contend that they can live fine without a man in their lives. While this may be true, there is also a negative side if it is not God's will for her. God may want her to have a husband, but she needs to allow Him to determine the right mate for her.

In our contemporary world, we see many black females resort to alternative means to combat or prevent much of the stress from relationships. In many cases, they are resorting to the practice of living together rather than marrying. This then gives them the option of easily exiting a bad relationship. This is a trick of Satan to destroy the honor and integrity of the black female. Unfortunately, Satan can be very good at concealing his deceptions..

Apparently, some churches even excuse cohabitating for the benefits of getting to know each other without the pain of divorce. I am appalled at supposedly Christian black females who condone such alliances. To identify oneself as a Christian and then condone sinful behavior is, to say the least, very sad. A Christian should not advocate cohabitating for any reason. The rationale behind such behavior is that the couple will be forgiven by God. While it's true that God loves us regardless of our weaknesses and shortcomings, this does not mean He will excuse immoral behavior. There are no two ways about it. It's sinful, and it's wrong. Shacking up will only lead to further identity problems.

Black females have become more amenable to cohabitation, duped into believing there is nothing spiritually wrong with it. Falsely, they believe that they can still maintain a healthy spiritual relationship with God while remaining in a sinful relationship. In the same way, lesbianism is on the rise. More and more black females are resorting to the deviant sexual behavior with other women to meet their sexual needs. In fact, I have known a couple of lesbian women who vehemently defended their life styles and argue that there is nothing immoral about their love for the same sex member. God has labeled this behavior an abomination. They believe that their individual freedom is all that matters, and every individual should do what is best for them. While this might seem attractive, the end result will be destructive. God says He will judge sin. Same sex relationships are not the solution to developing a strong self-awareness. Sin in any form destroys a person's inner beauty. Cohabitation and lesbianism will not aid the black woman's quest for identity, but will further erode the black family. It is another ploy of Satan to silently destroy her identity and spiritual purpose from God.

The black female must be careful in her efforts to attain a positive self-identity. Her desire to develop a strong self-image must not become clouded by standards and principles that are contrary to the Word of God. Although there is nothing wrong with every human desiring his or her own identity, the method used to obtain it is of great importance. The pursuit of self-awareness can lead to further negative consequences if it is not based on sound Christian principles and godly practices.

We must look at the black female coming out of the post slavery era. She emerged from slavery with a positive goal, and pursued it legitimately. History presents her as a spiritual heroine, and not a person who would use any means to achieve her intended goal. She focused on using integrity to find herself rather than doing her own thing. Our black female ancestors had character and integrity, which did not come cheap. Instead, she sought a spiritual closeness with God, high moral standards, and chose the Bible as her personal and family guide. In her efforts to pursue her own individual identity, often today's black female displays some similarities to slave women. However, she may not have calculated the cost of being spiritually free. Freedom has never been cheap; neither will it allow those who pursue it to escape without personal sacrifice.

The black female continues to make great strides and positive contributions in building strong and productive black families and neighborhoods. She has achieved financial success. Her management skills are to be applauded. No one can question the successfulness of the black female in the professional arena. However, as we examine the family structure, I find that much of the struggle within the black families can be directly traced to her desire to pursue financial and material success at the expense of family obligations. The pursuit of personal goals must cautiously be weighed to make sure not to jeopardize the family.

Several reports have raised concern about the stability of the black families, where both parents and especially mothers pursue personal goals above family commitments.

While I am not placing blame on the black female for the behavioral problems we are experiencing today, I believe the mothers' decision to pursue personal goals over family commitments in many cases has compounded the problem. However, nor am I advocating that all mothers should not work outside of the home to accomplish their personal dreams.

Gone are the days when children come home to find mom there. In most cases, children have no one there to give them direction and guidance. As a result, children are at great risk of deviant behavior. There are also those who wonder whether the mothers' decision to leave the home and seek personal fulfillment has not eroded the family's essential spiritual foundation. I applaud the black woman's effort to establish personal identity, but she must be careful not to overlook the need for a strong mother when children arrive home from school. This doesn't necessarily mean that homes where mothers are absent lead children to become deviants, but the risk is there. Each black family must determine whether there might be a greater risk to family stability if both parents are too often absent from home. There might just be a greater price to pay for selfishly focusing only on personal satisfaction. Overcrowded jails and prisons may be the result.

The road to personal achievement can't always be measured by financial gain and material goods. Today's black woman must assess the value of personal satisfaction. Is it worth the cost of losing her family? Her identity must not be measured by a career and professional success alone, but rather the internal joy of knowing that she is fulfilling the purpose and plan of God for her life.

The search for identity must be divinely driven and inspired, not secularly focused. Whether married, or unmarried, the black female should rely upon the Word of God to govern her dreams and guide her personal decisions and goals. Her ancestors understood the value of maintaining a godly self-image in a world determined to destroy her self-worth. Now that torch has been placed in her hands and it is up to her to help the black family stay intact.

This brings me to another issue the black female must come to terms with. The other day I read two articles on the changing roles of the black woman in the home. Interestingly enough, both of them focused upon the financial accomplishments of black women. Neither article spoke about the character and spiritual maturity of its subjects. I was personally disturbed by the type of photography and posture projected by the black women being featured as role models, examples of women who had achieved their personal goals. Yet, their dress and appearance did not represent the character of the woman that the word of God describes as virtuous and godly.

In particular, one magazine article highlighted a black woman displaying expensive jewelry and discussing her rise to stardom and affluence. The article emphasized success more than morals and godly principles. More and more disturbing circumstances like this one points to the fact that Blacks place too much emphasis on material goods and personal satisfaction rather than on godly living. The article was disturbing not because of its emphasis on the woman's success, but it never addressed character or lifestyle. Not a word was mentioned about her responsibility to model godliness to a sinful world.

Both women are in living arrangements with men outside of marriage. This sends a strong message to other young black women in pursuit of stardom that there is nothing wrong with cohabitating outside of marriage. This will contribute to poor self-image in these women. Falsely, they perceive of themselves as successful when in fact they still suffer from identity confusion. God values our behavior, but cares little about what we own. Godly behavior is a priceless value that we should all emulate.

My wife and I discussed black magazines and networks that do not portray the positive side of parenting and role modeling. I can pick up any black magazine to read about black women's problems but see photos of black females immodestly dressed. As sad as it is, my black sisters featured in such magazines might think they've made it. The truth is there is a certain hypocrisy here that needs to be dealt with. According to the world and its secular standards, this might seem fashionable. In reality, when black women seek to define their self-awareness by the amount of freedom they have to reveal flesh and strut their stuff, this leads to the destruction of the black family and the community.

Recently, I read a black published magazine that featured an article on violence, sex, and the hip-hop culture. The article focused on what the hip hop world had done to disrespect the black female, but missed the point that the pursuit of fame and fortune is the primary cause of disrespect. The time has come when black females must examine their own motives. There are huge drawbacks to success at any cost. The goal of most media outlets seems to be to expose enough of the black female's body to tantalize readers. I'm sure it sells magazines, but at what cost?

Black women criticize black rappers and men for gazing at their bodies. But if this is a problem, I would advise them to understand that revealing a physique in a magazine is being hypocritical. Without a doubt, the time has come when the black female must elect to seek for a modest and godly self-image, and denounce exhibitionism. I am often amazed at the conflicting standards staring back at me from a suggestive magazine or book cover while inside its articles call for men to stop lusting after the black female body and give her premiere respect.

Black females must take measures to promote respect for themselves. This is not to imply that black women as a race are all doing this; only that this is another indication of the black identity crisis. The question is--does the black race know who it really is? Do high moral standards and integrity really matter? Personal integrity should always rate above personal satisfaction. Thus, the black female needs to maintain her belief in integrity and self-respect. Her self-image should not be tarnished by pursuing a rise to secular stardom or quick success.

The Bible discusses "lasciviousness" as sexual exploitation or causing others to be tempted with lust. Black females are often used to market black glamour and beauty products. In most instances, they are little more than meat wagons, where their attire exposes the curves of their bodies. In fact, I have to wonder at times if bras are going to become extinct. Women on television are guilty of revealing entirely too much flesh. Almost any black magazine will have a woman pictured on the cover page revealing entirely too much of her body. They do not seem to be aware that they are sending a mixed message. This leads to a negative image and a lack of respect for her. We must ask ourselves this question: Do these images project a positive and godly self-image that will promote strong black family values and principles? Do they help our young black women understand and accept themselves as the spiritual vessels that God intended? Do they lead black males astray?

A healthy identity must derive from knowing God accepts her unconditionally and approves her because of her character, morals, and value system. The black female must demand greater respect for herself, and this includes refraining from being sold as a sex object. The hip-hop rap stars have had a part in soiling her image, but I believe she may be doing just as much damage by not holding onto the virtuous character qualities of her ancestors. Beauty is more than skin deep. Respect and spiritual character are vital to the black woman rediscovery of her real beauty and identity.

The Black Male-who is he?

Subsequent to the slave era, the black male was left both confused and without a real self-awareness. For decades he had been instructed how to think, when to think, and what to think about. Slavery ended, and he found himself with no identifiable role in a world of changes and progressive movements. Unlike the black female who got caught up in the Women Suffrage Movement, the black male had no national movement or progressive agent to help him survive the transitional changes taking place. Caught up in a world where he was not prepared to survive, the black man struggled to become recognized as a human, much less a man. He was seen as dumb, ignorant and incompetent. The plantation owners had done a magnificent job in convincing him that he was an insignificant thing.

The mass exodus of black men who left plantation life and headed to the cities discovered that the city offered industrial opportunity. Those who remained on the farms in the South became sharecroppers or field farmers. Later, they managed to buy small farms. The national and local political changes and struggles of the 1900's had a significant impact on the role and status of the black male. He obtained voting rights, got employment and even started a family. All these were positive image builders.

The black male had soon acquired at least a part of the freedom he had lost. He won the opportunity to become recognized as a human being. A few even became prosperous.

During the 1960's and 70's, the enrollment of black men in the colleges and universities increased significantly. They obtained better housing and employment opportunities and privileges. Black men entered politics on the local and national level. Although black men had entered the political world in the early part of the century, they had very little influence and power. The sixties and seventies saw a remarkable increase in the black man's role in the political sector. Along with all the positive changes came others that were not so positive. These included things like drugs, alcohol, sex, divorce, and high crime rates.

The black male's involvement with crime and drugs has hindered his identity development, stifling his God-intended purpose. Black men are believed to use more drugs than other races. Crime rates are higher in black neighborhoods, and a larger percentage of black males are incarcerated each day. He is more likely to find himself involved in violent crime, and is more than likely to be convicted than other races. He is more likely to have poor health and will face more long-term health problems than other nationalities. His family has a much greater probability of living without him because of sickness, divorce or death. Taken together, these concerns add up to big problems for the black male and his identity, and they will not help his current situation at all. The absence of most black males as spiritual servant leaders in their homes has done tremendous damage to the Black race. When mother, Johnny and the rest of the family goes off to church, his dad in most cases remains at home. This causes additional identity crisis for children. From what I have observed, most of our black men are spectators during a time when they need to be in the church to quarterback the family through worship service.

Considering all the negative press that the black man is more likely to desert his family, will do nothing to improve his image. He is almost certainly to suffer from more rejection each time he fails to demonstrate that he is reliable as a father and husband. Along with the high number of black men being incarcerated, each incident where a family is left without a dependable male harms his identity. And when we add to this that each time the black family is left to fend for itself without him, his self esteem will worsen. Not only this but also our black sisters are emotionally, spiritually and economically impacted. Taken together this all spells trouble for the black family. The black male cannot afford to have his image tarnished any more than it already is. He is in desperate need of a makeover in his identity. The future of the black family and its survival is depending upon black men to rise up and fulfill their purpose in Christ.

With so many family problems confronting him, he is often overwhelmed. Facing these family issues can cause him to become unstable and unreliable without strong encouragement. As a result, divorce is highly likely. In fact, his reputation for fleeing a long-term marriage is notorious. More and more the black female finds herself threatened by slavery much different than that on the plantation.

The black male is no longer forced to abdicate his family role by the white plantation owners. His choice to divorce and separate from his family is his own. A new form of slavery called self-destruction threatens the black family and can rob the black man of his dignity and stability. The freedom to indulge his lusts makes him his own worst enemy. With freedom comes increased accountability and responsibility. Too many of us have failed both of these tests. We desperately need to improve in order to help the future generation avoid making the same mistakes we made.

At a time when all black men need to stand and be counted, many have chosen to pursue a different form of identity. This segment has made a decision to pursue those things that are pleasurable for a season. God calls these things sins. With sinful pleasure always come the consequence of self-degradation and destruction.

We as black males owe our black ancestors a great debt of gratitude for paving the way for future achievement. They died so the black male would know that God loves him, too, and has an identity for him just like any other nationality. Those stalwarts of the past would not want black men to be negatively identified. Instead, they would want the world to know that their struggles were not in vain. They would be devastated to see what time has done to the image and identity of black people, and especially the black male.

Some years ago the popular slogan "I'm black and I'm proud," meant something other than mere words. This slogan supported the sincere belief that God intended every race to have self-respect. This pride went far deeper than skin color. It was born out of the recognition that a people willing to live by godly principles would ultimately overcome. There was a sense that "I am someone not because of what I have, but whose I am." The endorsers of that slogan saw themselves as having a respectable identity, endowed by God. Without a doubt, the black freedom fighters of the past relied upon faith in God and a determination to survive an oppressive system. Somewhere between then and now, many black males lost sight of that vision.

Far too many black men today live for pleasure, emphasizing temporal things and devaluing the values that matter to God.

Dr. Martin Luther King had a dream, but will black people let it die? All too often, the black race seems to be going in the opposite direction from that dream, which is evidence that some of his dream was never understood nor accepted. He did not emphasize external values, but internal changes that would produce positive self-awareness and long term well-being.

In general, too many black men, like black women seem to feel that success is measured by wealth. Many black men identify with Hollywood figures, sport jocks, and entertainment personalities. Young black boys learn how to play sports long before they understand the value of more important facets of life. They will go to the basketball court, even though they have difficulty spelling the word. Parents allow these black young boys to play with their friends before checking to see how they are doing in school. I do not mean to imply that all black parents do this. Just that too many young black males fall behind right under their parents' noses.

Further, young black males receive less discipline today than at any other time in history. This should concern every black person, because it is critical. Some family sociologists agree that too many black parents are not consistent in their discipline practices. Teachers and administrators agree that black males are growing up with disciplinary problems that are ignored. Each day we learn of the increasing number of young teenage black males being murdered in the D.C.

Metro area. This morning I heard on my car radio that five black teenage males were murdered in Washington D.C. within the past two weeks.

In many cases, teachers can't get the parental support necessary to maintain order in the classroom. Some parents defend the disciplinary problems of their children while teachers desperately struggle to maintain a good learning environment.

A large number of young males today dress to identify with hip hop superstars and not as productive members of society. Clearly, they do not understand that their appearance can harm the image they should portray. Young men whose pants hang off their backsides are not respecting themselves. I have discussed this subject with several young black males, and they do not believe this defines what they stand for. Surprisingly many black parents believe that attire should not be a big concern. They fail to realize that these young people will become identified with those who are violent, and they will be labeled accordingly.

Contrary to what we might believe, society identifies us by the company we keep and our appearance.

Needless to say, this image has left the black race with an unwanted stigma. Supermarkets, malls and other public establishments are leery and distrustful of black males who look like thugs. In other words, the black male who seeks to be recognized for his individual ability and intelligence cannot expect the society to applaud him when his appearance is frightening and his character deplorable. Blacks cannot continue to blame others for our failure to train and take seriously our parental responsibilities. Johnnie should be at home with his parents and not hanging out on street corners. Unfortunately, too many black parents allow their children to grow up much too soon. In other words, they have so much freedom that discipline becomes extremely difficult, if not impossible. Although many Black parents are strict with their children, more need to place logical restrictions on their children's freedom.

When growing up in the South as a young boy, my mother told me to carry myself so that others would not perceive me as a bad boy. In this way she taught me to have self-respect. I remember both my parents teaching me the importance of having dignity and character. My father was a proud black man who would not tolerate nonsense from his children. He would tell us, "We have never been inside a jail, so don't expect us to come and get you if you get into trouble and end up there." Do I believe they would have helped us? Who knows, but my sisters and brothers were unwilling to risk getting into trouble by identifying with the wrong element. We worked hard to make our parents proud.

Of all races, Blacks can least afford social and moral rejection. The black male emerged from slavery, as difficult as it was, with his dignity intact. The institution of slavery did not destroy his value system. Instead he learned how to handle anger and avoid self-destructive behaviors. Today, many black males are on the verge of destroying themselves through association with violence. They must learn to deal with unpleasant circumstances with maturity. Peaceful solutions and long suffering paid off for our ancestors. Their goal was to get out of slavery and into freedom. Today the black male has freedom, but too many abuse it.

Coming out of slavery, he struggled to gain recognition. Many escaped poverty, but have yet to discover that the road to success is not paved with gold. And while there is nothing innately wrong with wealth, it cannot impart dignity. Only God can help the black male discover real character, self-love, and respect. Dr. King's dream had no place for social and moral rejection, but it had lots of room for love and forgiveness. It was his character and love that defined who this man really was. He understood the struggle of the black male. Nevertheless, he understood that society does not define who a man is, but he defines himself through his character and purpose in God.

As a black male, I understand the struggle to be accepted by society, but I refuse to accept violence as a means to that end. Dr. King's message left us with a clear path to follow, so let's get to it.

The black man's quest for freedom must be based on an internal desire for positive character. His identity depends upon his identification with God. Jesus said, "I have come that you might have life, and have it more abundantly." That means that you and I can have an abundant life according to God's purpose for each one of us. It does not mean He wants the black man to carve out a purpose and plan for himself. It does not mean he must pick up a gun and rob a bank to be strong. Neither does it mean that sexual conquests are the measure of manhood. God has already offered us strength through the personal sacrifice of his Son, Jesus Christ (Phil. 4:13). Focusing on things of the world will blind a man to his spiritual purpose. Jesus wants all men to depend upon Him for their personal significance.

Perhaps the greatest error we make is focusing on accumulating things that lead to self-destruction instead of positive self-awareness. Jesus has already mapped out a plan so each of us could enjoy fulfillment. We have many options, but only God's plan will satisfy us.

In John 14:6 Jesus said, "I am the way, the truth, and the life, no man comes to the father but by me." Perhaps you are thinking, but I don't believe in that religion thing. Neither do I believe in a religion thing, but in what Jesus called the abundant life. Further, I believe in trusting Christ as the means to an abundant life, a life that satisfies. Things will rot and decay. People are going to die and leave us. But Jesus offers a peaceful life even in the midst of a chaotic world order. Self-reliance is not the way to an abundant spiritual life. It can only be obtained through a personal relationship with Jesus Christ. If you attempt to use guns and drugs to obtain self-awareness, it will not last and eventually you will end up either jailed or dead. God loves and cares for black men. However, the black male must accept this love as truth.

Too many black men make the mistake of seeking self-worth in their own way, seeing Christianity as a sign of weakness, and they misunderstand who Jesus is. They believe the theology that when Jesus said to "turn the other cheek" He was weak. They believe it is a sign of great strength to take what you want. Not only black males, but all men must learn to trust God to help them experience self-esteem and importance. We can't get our value from other people; it must come from God himself. Feelings and people are fickle. Haven't you known friends that said they would always be there for you? Then you discover that they forgot you ever existed. You can have lots of "stuff," but it's all only temporary. Only Jesus Christ is dependable.

Man may treat you according to the color of your skin, but Jesus does not see color, He sees our needs. Therefore, every black male needs Jesus. We've all experienced prejudice. But this is no reason for Blacks to reject God and His plan. The more we seek an intimate relationship with Christ, the less we will struggle with identity problems, because His identity will begin to rise up in us. Having an identity is not dependent upon working or strategizing, but upon trusting in Jesus Christ. This, my friend, is the beginning of getting and keeping your identity.

Genesis 1:27 says all men have been created in the image of God. This image was restored through the sacrificial death of Christ. The goal of the black male should be to fulfill the will of God through relationship with Christ. Identity has its origin in the word "identify." In this case it means that we identify with Jesus Christ as our source of life. And if we identify with Him through accepting His plan and purpose for life, we will take on His identity.

Jesus never had to worry about his identity. Did other people try to define who He was? Yes, they even went as far as defining His disciples. One day Jesus asked Peter, "Who do you say that I am?" Jesus was not concerned with what men said about him. He wanted Peter to identify with him so that he would have a strong identity as the servant of Christ. Later, Peter would be challenged regarding his identity with Jesus.

Someday you and I will, too. Only Christ can give the black male the self-confidence necessary to live in a world where forces work to destroy his sense of significance. There are black men who seem to have good self-esteem, but this will not last unless based on God's opinion of them. Success is not a true measurement of positive self-esteem. These men still need Jesus to confirm who they really are, because if the world sets their value it will not last.

Black men must learn to walk away from negative images and forces that lead then away from a covenant relationship with God. They should not tolerate or exalt lewd behavior. Instead they should look for opportunities to adopt traits that cause others to see them in a different spiritual light.

Dr. King did not become the man he did just because of the color of his skin or his masculinity, but by the spirit and might of the omniscient, omnipresent and omnipotent Creator God.

Today's black male is too often identified as a baby-producing machine that hops from bed to bed. This kind of image will do nothing to help him build a strong and positive identity.

Illegitimate birth rates continue to skyrocket. The number of graves filled by black males continues to rise. There is a trend where black males adopt an alternative bisexual lifestyle called "on the down low," which allows for relationships with both men and women. This behavior will not help the black male to feel better about who he is. While this may appear to be an expression of individuality, it will produce undesired consequences. Because of these behaviors the chances for survival are lower for young black males than for any other race.

As was mentioned earlier, black males have more health problems than any other race. Chances are good he will die at a much younger age than other men. These statements should sound an alarm that we are in a life-threatening identity crisis and must wake up before it is too late. Black men today have made great strides and positive accomplishments, but we have a long way to go.

We must call attention to the alarming number dying from lack of wisdom and knowledge. Many of us have no clue what our real problem is. We give little thought to why we were born, why we are here. Too many of us think we are here to have fun or be fulfilled with pleasure. As long as self-serving behaviors dictate the way many black men live their lives, nothing will change.

Today prisons overflow with violent black men. Although the black race makes up less than twenty percent of the overall population, black men commit the highest percentage of crimes. Prison life will not erase this self-esteem problem. Coming out of prison, many former inmates do not shake the inmate image, and end up going back within a year or two after release. They have not learned to avoid the bad influences that imprisoned them in the first place. Many are released and discover that society does not welcome them back. Unable to deal with the challenges once released, they can actually become more resentful toward those on the outside. In most cases they will return to places they know.

From adolescence, the young black male is encouraged to "score" or have sex to prove his masculinity. Others in his environment boast about their conquests. He is isolated and rejected unless he proves his worth to his peers. During slavery, the black male slaves were deemed valuable depending upon the number of female slaves they could impregnate. The more females he could impregnate the greater his value to the plantation owner. Within the slave community he was highly regarded for his virility. As a result, the black male slave discovered he had value and saw it as a way of becoming useful. His sexual ability made him feel significant and gave him an identity, even though he was being exploited. At least, he believed he had significance.

Not much has changed since the slave era. The black male continued to search for an identity. Sexual conquests became a mean to acquire status and be needed. The idea that sexual dominance equals power has destroyed many black families.

Today, many black males are often discontented with one female, and this attitude has devastating results. His sexual appetites dictate his behavior. Sex becomes no different than a drink of water, quenching his thirst for the moment, but must be satisfied over and over again. Black men who practice this behavior are caught in a web of lies, deceit and emptiness. They will eventually discover, often too late, that they have been betrayed by their own lust. I Peter 2:11

instructs man to flee youthful lust and abstain from it because it leads to self-destruction. Such men actually want to obtain their identity through sexual gratification but are deceived, believing that sex is the answer, when, in truth, they are enslaved by their behavior. In the end, these black men will feel degraded and insignificant.

In many cases, this vicious struggle ends with HIV infection, and eventually a diagnosis of AIDS. As I watched a recent democratic presidential debate, the candidates addressed the devastation of black families by AIDS. They mentioned that Black women are twice as likely as other races to get AIDS. Black men are twice as likely to end up with it and get little medical assistance. As I sat and listened to the debate, I realized the real problem is not just a lack of money to treat AIDS, but that Blacks have not accepted responsibility to change their behavior.

Clearly we must teach our youth that engaging in extramarital sex is morally unholy and unacceptable to God as well as a deadly game of roulette.

Many Blacks feel they are free to enjoy themselves, that their sexuality is none of anyone else's business. And this attitude is not limited to Blacks. The problem with selfishness is that it destroys lives, their own and others'. Then, many black people feel that if only black men would use condoms this would eliminate the devastation caused by AIDS. While I agree that the use of condoms might help prevent the spread of infection, it still does not change the psychological and spiritual impact of extramarital sex. Neither will it address the long-term identity problem within the black community. In addition, premarital sex robs youth of their virginity. God intended sex to be reserved until a man and woman come together in holy matrimony. In addition, men who seek significance through sex will have destroyed other lives in their ignorance.

Many black men seek to escape the pressures of life by using drugs and alcohol. These vices will not satisfy the craving for identity and like sex must be repeated over and over again. Drug use is responsible for much of the AIDS deaths, and contributes to the breakdown of the family. A walk in the back alleys of the inner cities will reveal that far too many black males are addicted to drugs. Some are already infected with the HIV virus, or soon will be unless they receive help to overcome the habit.

Just like drugs and sex, alcohol is also used as an escape from the problems of low esteem and loneliness and can be very addictive. Attempting to use vices to escape pain is not the answer. Jesus said, "Come unto me all ye who are heavy laden, and I will give you rest." We cannot find rest at the end of a needle, in a bed with strange women, or in a bottle of liquor. These offer promises they cannot keep. They dull the pain temporarily, but only lead to deeper loneliness and emptiness. Death can be physical or spiritual. In either case, the black male who looks for his identity here will end up another disillusioned statistic. Until he reaches that pivot point in his life where he turns to God for help, he will remain unfulfilled.

Identity problems are not limited to any particular race. On the 16th of April 2007, the world was shocked when a young man at Virginia Tech University had made his way into the history books by shooting down fellow students. After his killing spree, he took his own life. Why would he commit such a heinous act of violence?

Why would a young Asian man, from a usually non-violent race, commit such a terrible crime? Thirty-two hurting families and the world were left to mourn the worst mass murder a university had ever seen. This young man had some history of disturbed behavior, and yet no one knew his mental state made him capable of murder. We may never know what drove him to such extremes. But we do know that something went very wrong.

The most frightening thing about this incident is the fact that violence can take place at anytime, anywhere, with any race. The Virginia Tech tragedy is another example of the desperate need to help each other establish a personal identity through encouragement and mutual recognition. There is no justification for what this young man did to others, but, clearly no one ever got close enough to see his need for help. His roommate and others, including teachers saw his strange behavior, but none considered him a threat. The question is: Would it have made a difference if someone had sought him out and talked with him one on one? We will never know the answer to that question now.

The evening of that incident, I realized that we often fail to see the problems troubling those around us. And when we do, perhaps we are too busy to spend a few moments to reach out to them. And though no one is responsible for someone else's self-image, it helps to know others care. In addition, the more we understand God loves us, the less likely we are to destroy others.

Although we cannot change the outcome of that dreadful day, we can become more sensitive to the needs of those around us for love and acceptance. It was obvious to me that the problem of that gunman did not start that day at Blacksburg, Virginia, but during his childhood. No one listening to the tape he left behind would disagree that he was in desperate need of help.

As I ponder this madness, I must examine myself to see how I can help others feel they belong in a world where we are little more than numbers. The lesson to be learned from this violent act is when people lack an understanding and appreciation of themselves they are more likely to become a menace to society. The behavior they demonstrate is always out of line with what is normal. Such a person's view of life is distorted, and his dreams and goals become lost in the rage that silently eats away at his core. The truth is there are hurting people all around us, but we are often too busy to notice. The high crime rate that we are experiencing today is a direct result of Blacks who have a very poor self-image that only God can correct. Instead of casting their cares on the Lord, these people have gone another way.

The scripture says, "Cast all your cares upon me, for I care for you" (I Peter 5:7). What a tragedy that the gunmen at Virginia Tech did not understand the spiritual value of carrying everything to God in prayer. Without a doubt there are people who feel they have no way of escape. Because they do not belong to Jesus Christ, they live life from day to day with absolutely no healthy expectation. Gang members in most cases are people who look to belong and be accepted. They are drawn to the criminal subculture as an alternative means of achieving significance. Individuals that are part of these gangs are there because they do not feel like productive member of our society. Researchers and counselors have proven that no matter what racial group a person belongs to, if he feels a sense of belonging and acceptance he is less likely to get caught up in a life of crime.

Helping others feel a sense of accomplishment is not an easy task. Years of low expectations and a lack of encouragement can do severe damage. Left uncorrected, discouragement and hopelessness can lead to violence. Gone are the days when we can ignore people with problems. No man is an island unto himself. Though we are not responsible for anyone else's mental health, we can help others discover their value in God's plan.

I often ponder the reasons people go to such extremes to resolve conflicts; some will stop short of nothing less than total destruction. The Middle East conflict demonstrates the importance of and need for using peaceful means to resolve conflicts. An Islamic extremist group believes that violence paves the way for success. Years of fighting have proven the fallacy of such thinking. Even spending billions of dollars has not put an end to war and violence.

Regardless of race or nationality people need to learn to resolve their differences peacefully and not through violence and retribution. Unforgiveness prevents peaceful resolution to any problem, and perpetuates violence. Violence cannot bring peace, but the love of Christ can.

When Cain slew Abel, he was struggling with an identity crisis. He felt inferior to his brother because God accepted his brother's sacrifice and rejected his. God gave him a chance to claim his God-given blessing by bringing the proper sacrifice, but instead his jealousy got the best of him and ultimately, destroyed him.

"Blessed are the peacemakers, for they shall inherit the earth." God has a covenant with everyone who pursues peace through Christ. In John 16:33 Jesus said we would find our peace in Him. In I Peter 3:11, the Word tells us to seek peace and pursue it.

Blacks can only overcome their problems with the proper attitude and altitude with God. In I Corinthians 14:33 Paul said Jesus is the author of peace. This peace can only be received from a covenant relationship with Jesus Christ.

What is a covenant? Biblically speaking, it is a binding agreement entered into by one or more individuals. It is not joining a gang or clique. God desires a covenant relationship with us so we do not resort to destructive means to feel a sense of significance. The failure to enter a covenant relationship with God leaves a person seeking alternative self-centered means to feel complete and useful. The covenant relationship with God means we take on God's identity and image; we believe His opinion that we are important, we matter. Character modeled after Christ's character leads to a very strong self-awareness.

We do not reach spiritual goals in our own strength, but rather when we learn to relinquish our plans and allow God to mold our character according to His divine plan. So what is the best means to achieve a strong identity in this present world? First of all, it's only available through relationship with Christ. Second, stop blaming others for your failure and lack of achievement. Instead, trust God to help you become the person you are destined to be. Contemporary Blacks must take a page from the books of their ancestors. They knew God had an appointed destiny for each of them.

Apostle Paul said, "Let this mind be in you that was also in Christ Jesus" (Philippians 2:5). As incredible as it might seem, this verse holds the key to knowing who you are. Jesus never had an identity problem. When the Pharisees and his opponents sought to label Him according to their particular brand of legalism, He rejected their opinions, in favor of God's opinion, the only one that mattered. In addition, He challenged them to define themselves by His Father's will.

Jesus did not have to convince Himself who He was, because God had already given Him His identity. Too many believers go around trying to identify ourselves via a world's system that has absolutely nothing to offer us. Thus, Jesus accepted His divinity and nothing man could do or say could shake His self-confidence. Black people need to stop letting their peers, family or friends define who they are. If there's one thing we should have grasped from the slave era, it is the fact that if we do not know our purpose, others will mistakenly define it for you. Unfortunately, many Blacks today seem to have placed themselves back into this box by trying to fit in. Our black brothers who end up in prison make a choice to disregard the principles and standards of God. Instead, they choose to focus on get-rich-quick schemes and pleasures.

Their love is for the world, not for God. Placing our value into the hands of others allows them control over us. To know who we are in Christ, we must submit to God, admitting that we don't know what is best for us. A case in point: Some time ago a young man shared with me his struggle regarding the opinions of others. He said he was a born again believer, but disagreed with those who shared their faith with others. He felt this was unnecessary. He kept his faith and work separate.

He did not keep a Bible at work because he felt it would hinder his chances of advancing in the workplace. In this particular case, he was giving his supervisor, and not God whom he claimed to love, control over his destiny. He said one thing with his voice, but his lifestyle was controlled by a secular value system. He went on to say that he feared others would think that he was a religious fanatic. Finally, he said that his race made him uncomfortable about sharing his faith with his peers. Clearly he suffered from an identity crisis.

I also recall meeting a young lady who decided to have sex because of peer pressure. Her plan was to go to law school, but unfortunately she got involved with a young man who claimed he really loved her. He convinced her to sleep with him in order to prove her love. As is often the case she became pregnant and her plans to go to law school had to be postponed. Unfortunately for her, she had given another person control over her identity.

Both of these cases show what can happen when we allow others to define us. We're all tempted to go to others for positive reinforcement, but a godly self-image depends on letting God define who we are. Each day Blacks interact with a world that helps shape the person they will become. Ultimately, the choice they make is up to them. The stronger we feel about who we are, the more we can contribute to society.

We are all influenced by our surroundings. There were times in my youth when I was confused as to who I should become. Growing up in the South caused me to ask myself, why did God make Blacks less valuable than other races? I didn't really believe this, but since I lived in a cultural setting where this myth was fostered, it was easy to buy into the lie. The South during that time devalued the contribution of Blacks to society. Yet, I attended church and studied about God, who is no respecter of persons.

Further, I was surrounded with few people who could influence me toward my God-given identity. I questioned the authority of those who made and sanctioned laws that discriminated against people based on color or gender. But my parents often told me not to question those in authority because it would lead to trouble. They were afraid I could be one of the southern Blacks who ended up hanging from a tree or drowned in a river somewhere. At that time Blacks were not allowed to drink from White water fountains or enter restaurants through front doors, and to buck the tide was costly.

Yet, here I was living in a country that actually defended this system as the will of God. Even today there are those who continue to perpetuate these myths.

For years, I suffered from an inferior complex and never felt accepted. It is only by the mercy of God that my self-image was not destroyed. It was several years after becoming a man that I realized that I had placed my identity in the hands of those who wanted me to fail. Once I accepted God's opinion of me, my pain subsided.

During the summer I graduated from high school, I was blessed with a job with the Chipley, Florida social services. While there I worked with a wonderful white woman by the name of Mrs. Gilbert, who had much to do with boosting my self-esteem. Though she was not my immediate supervisor, she would spend time encouraging me to believe in myself regardless to what others thought of me. My immediate supervisor was also a Caucasian lady, but she did not care for Blacks. Determined to complete my summer work there, I focused on my work and became more confident that I could stay on that job in spite of the fact that my supervisor would have liked to have seen me fail. Because of my special mentor who had confidence in me, I made a decision to overcome my adversities. I learned to depend on God. Those experiences in the South caused me to search the Bible for my strength. My sense of significance grew despite negative past experiences because I felt of value to my creator, God.

Subsequent to developing a deeper faith in God, I learned that the key to maintaining ones identity is to forgive others and forget negative comments said about you. Many people identify with unpleasant memories and experiences from their past. If you happen to belong to the Black race, you are twice as likely to experience low self-esteem. But does this mean that being Black condemns you to poor self-identity? Absolutely not! Genesis 3:27 says that you have been wonderfully made in His own image. So what others say about you is merely their opinion, not the truth. No matter what your nationality or race, you bear the image of an excellent and sovereign God. Race and gender have nothing to do with your value and significance in this life. This truth will help Blacks overcome their identity crisis. Once they comprehend the truth that only God assigns value to them, opinions fade in importance.

Black men are not to envision themselves based upon any other evaluation than the Word of God. God is accessible to all regardless of race. It is our responsibility to seek and bind the truth of God deep into our hearts. Having the character of Christ is essential to identity, because it offers hope to us all.

Jesus said, "So as a man thinketh, so is he." If a man thinks wrong thoughts about himself, and never outgrows them, he will be socially and spiritually affected. Further he will believe what others perceive about him, whether it is truth or not. When we trade our own misperceptions about our identity for the truth of God, we become conquerors. As Black men gain increased scriptural wisdom they will become vessels of hope and love for others. When black parents love themselves, they model how to love and be loved. God is a God of love, and no man can remain unloving after getting to know Him.

THIRTEEN

Moving Beyond Blackness

Contemporary Black America is at a great crossroad. Blacks are confronted by new challenges each day. It is impossible to avoid criticism entirely. Thus, we must learn how to deal with it. Jesus did. And not only did He deal with it, but He also taught His disciples the importance of not defining themselves by the people and customs of that day. Jesus spent much of his time teaching and training his disciples to get to know Him, and the Father, defining their identity apart from the world. Blacks must move beyond blackness and rely on God's image to define them. Jesus refused to allow others to define his character, but identified with his Father's will. Blacks should grasp the importance of doing likewise.

A Communication Breakdown

Though the quality of life has improved for Blacks, we still hear derogatory slang used to describe us. Words such as "nigger" and "spook" have been used since slavery days. Recently the NAACP held its 98th annual convention, and one of its primary focus was "How to remove the N word from our vocabulary." The use of this word grew out of the evil institution of slavery, but it has refused to die in present day America. During slavery, Caucasians used this word to identity a black person. However, subsequent to the slave era, this word migrated and Blacks began to use it in conversation. Its original meaning was intended to describe someone who was considered "worthless and no account." This word was used in a negative context to symbolize disrespect. White plantation owners first used it to make a profound effect on its victims.

The impact of the "N word" was symbolic of the life of a slave. It robbed the slave of his value and self esteem. Referring to slaves as no good permanently destroyed much of their self-image.

The beginning of life originated with God who gave man value and self worth. While it is literally impossible to measure the psychological and social damage of insults, research confirms significant damage to the identity of one who is constantly belittled.

An infant is assigned value at birth, but this is quickly reversed if he is humiliated and rejected.

The only hope the slave had to maintain his dignity was his family. But families were soon separated, stripping the slave of what identity he had. The only encouragement he received came from other slaves. As strange as this may sound, it was his birth image that gave the slave some reason to exist. He knew that God made him, was with him, and would eventually deliver him out of his predicament. How did he hold onto that hope apart from the family? Slaves reminded each other of their roots.

Emerging from slavery with a negative stigma was not only bad for Blacks, but for the entire country. The colonists had fled to America seeking an identity apart from the one England assigned them. Ironically, this pursuit of independence was a dream denied to the slaves. The fallout from those efforts haunts Blacks even until today.

Blacks have come a long way from the slave era. Many have carved out a piece of the good life for themselves. Churches and organizations like the NAACP have been at the forefront calling for progressive changes. Books have been written, and magazine articles published on the black struggle for identity. Although progress has been made, Black wounds still fester. Did America fail the black people during the slavery era? Yes, it did. But what have we done to help rectify this tragic situation?

Time for a Reality Check

Sometimes we launch efforts to correct the past without fully understanding how we got there in the first place. I applaud the NAACP efforts to take positive action to bury the "N word." However, in order to be successful we must go beyond a mock funeral. We need a mind transformation. Blacks must come to understand that permanent burial of negative language must start at home.

We must forever bury our derogatory slang. We must demand a permanent end of all offensive language, boycotting television networks, radio programs and the hip hop and R&B cultures that use these words to make big money. Ironically, the Hollywood image appeals to the same Blacks who complain that Whites see them the same way they did in the Jim Crow era. As long as the fashion and entertainment industries focus on selling garbage to a people they perceive loves to purchase it, very little will change. The change must start with our mindset.

It is essential that a conversion take place in our belief system. We cannot afford to continue to append the belief that making money is more important than protecting and conserving the identity of a people. We must boycott venues where women expose themselves and shake their backsides in videos, as well as the hip hop culture that identifies black women as ho's and bitches. For too long, black people have made the wrong choices and refused to see them as problems. Blame belongs on those of us who perpetuate the problem. Some Blacks feel it's okay to use such language within our race, but that does nothing to correct the root problem. We must no longer condone such things; it must stop now. Our love for each other must outweigh our love for materialism, power and entertainment.

Before we can expect others to respect us, we must learn to respect ourselves. This starts with recognizing that the easy route to success contains many deceptive roadblocks. Character qualities like love, respect and dignity will build up the black race to reach higher than ever before.

We have become a race that encourages people to pursue their dreams at any cost. Too often we fail to teach our young people that unless we cling onto values like integrity and dignity, allowing God to be first place in our hearts, we will forever lose our identity. God is the only source of joy and satisfaction.

Any lasting change must be cumulative. Along with the funeral for the "N word," we must also bury the belief that freedom means doing whatever we want. Permanent change can take place, but we can only earn respect from ourselves and others when we do what is right in the sight of God. The Apostle Paul was correct when he said, "I am what I am by the grace of God." The best image enhancement tool is God and His imprint on each of our souls.

One day Jesus said, "In me you will have peace" (John 16:33). What an incredible assurance in a world that does not know peace, because it does not know the God of peace. In I Peter 3:11, we are told to seek peace and pursue it." In I Corinthians 14:33, Paul defines Jesus as the "Author of peace." The issues facing the black population today can only be resolved through peaceful means through the power of God.

There are a few mandatory initiatives that I believe black people should take to step out of their current struggles. If you are one of those individuals who think Blacks are doing fine, consider this: the Word of God tells us there is no way to achieve excellence apart from salvation through Jesus Christ.

While a percentage of Blacks are doing great and considered to be very successful, others are less fortunate. Apparently, more people than ever are confusing wealth with success. But a closer look at the condition of the world will prove that no matter how rich or famous someone is, without a relationship in Christ to grant wisdom he will soon perish. Only those who grasp this truth are truly successful.

We are blessed to live in a country with great wealth. But too many Blacks live in poor and disappointing communities. These do not have strong positive outlooks and high expectations. Their lives are riddled with despair and deprivation.

I recently saw a news story about small black children. When asked to choose beautiful toy dolls, they did not choose Black dolls, but selected white dolls. The black children saw themselves as having less value because of their race. The tragedy of this is that they are likely to go through life feeling the same way. And this perception of what is of value cannot be corrected unless we as adults help counteract such negative messages. Children learn their significance from their parents and their surroundings.

FOURTEEN

Long Term Consequences of Low Self-Esteem

All of us have challenges in life that if left unresolved can lead to serious handicap. From our childhood we accumulate a vast number of life experiences, many which cause us hurt and pain. The longer they go unresolved, the more damage occurs. Over the years, we learn to bury our needs, hide our pain, conceal the problem areas, cope with the hurt, and fear the unknown or sense of helplessness and expectations. We do this because it is what everyone seems to expect of us. Yet, we go through life incomplete and unhealed. Although we are aware that we have unmet needs within, we have little understanding as to how to overcome them, and become healed.

We live in a contemporary world where we are consumed by pressure, expectations, responsibilities and job related stress. Most of us do our best to function. If we feel we have no way out, we become overloaded. In general, Blacks respond just like any other race of people. Feeling unable to fit in with our culture or society, we end up reacting with angry, pretense, or apathy. This causes us to feel guilty, and maybe even resentful. So what happens next when this occurs? We are forced to handle these emotions, but with no idea how to handle and overcome these feelings deep within our souls.

The ideal world would have been that we grew up in a culture with equal opportunities, resources and self awareness. If we had grown up in a perfect society with as much love and nurturing as necessary, perhaps life would make more sense. Think about this for a moment. If those

Blacks that seem to suffer from a lack of self respect, value and respect for others, had never been physically, mentally or emotionally confused, subjected to negative words, betrayed, or neglected and rejected, maybe the consequences would be somewhat different. But since imperfect people and circumstances can have a dramatic impact upon the person we become, especially during our formative years, we end up imperfect individuals. While some Blacks manage to escape the negative impact from these life experiences, others do not.

Those Blacks that have learned to recognize the drawback from clinging to bad life experiences are more likely to turn to God instead of away from him. When we fully surrender to the omnipotent God, he alone will provide us with words of truth, love and encouragement. I don't believe that any person that comes to God will be rejected or mistreated. He will not speak negative unkind words that belittle or degrade us because of our skin color or gender. Jesus promised to never leave nor forsaken us. But you and I must first come to him. The Bible says, "Come unto me all ye that labor and are heavy laden, and I will give you rest" (Matt. 11:28). What an invitation to us all to surrender our hurts and pain. The only factor that prevents the healing power and love of God to us is our failure to surrender our souls to him. The following long-term consequences can lead to low self-esteem.

A Damaged Soul

Our minds are the battlefields where we engage war with Satan. It is this part of us that strongly needs to be revived. The negative experiences in life such as racism, self hate and anger impact our self-esteem. Thus, in order to overcome the damage inflicted to us, we must surrender our soul to God instead of rejecting him. The consequence of failing to do so is costly. The word instructs us "Do not be conformed to this world-this age that is not always fair and equitable. But be ye transformed (changed) by the renewing of your mind. Why do we need to renew our minds? It is because of all the negative words, hurt, and harm that can harbor there. This is necessary in order to prove what is that good and acceptable and perfect will of God" (Romans 12:1, 2). Victory to a healthy self image in Blacks rests with them adopting this biblical truth principle. Unless the damaged soul is shattered, complete healing and self-awareness can never be accomplished.

Childhood Leftover Trauma

A majority of trauma is sustained from things that happened to us even from those formative years and may not be changed. Blacks were subjected to slavery. It would be great if we could somehow reverse the clock, and that period of history deleted. However, this will not occur. Because of the traumatic experiences in everyone's life, not just Blacks, we end up with unmet needs, hurts, and unresolved crises from birth. It is these areas of vulnerabilities that cause fear, anxiety and doubt that prevent us from submitting to an intimate relationship with God. Have you ever tried to witness to someone and felt their fear and doubt that God could really help them?

Those unmet needs, unhealed hurts and other crises of your life fight against you surrendering your life to God. Regardless of how much witnessing about God's abundant love we share with Blacks harboring a damaged soul, they will not readily accept our testimony. These have suffered too long from the trauma of childhood experiences. The eroding decay of their unmet needs, hurts, and pain eat away at their infrastructure-the soul. A traumatic childhood takes a long time, if not a life time to be erased. Then, there are some that will not rise above their fears and hate. They become the black men, women and youth that choose a life of violence and substance abuse.

Many Blacks end up appeasing their flesh needs through destructive solutions. We think if I had more money, a different spouse, a better paying job, a better appearance or new car, I would be a happier person. But the truth is that none of these things can fill our emotional and spiritual needs. Only God can give value from our life experience of being devalued.

Subsequent to attempting to bury our hurts and pain, we retaliate against those we feel responsible. When this happens, we find ourselves so to speak, like a dog chasing its tail. The problem is our unmet needs will not be crucified by hiding them; they must be surrendered to God. If not, they lie down for a moment, but come back to frustrate us. We may try to bury them with the offerings of other alternatives like food, sex, drugs, multiple marriages or cohabitating in immoral relationships. But they will get out of their graves and prance back again. When we surrender them to God by renewing our minds in his word, we avoid the trauma of unmet needs, hurts and unresolved pain.

Wrong Desires and Actions

Each day we read the newspapers and listen to the news on television, we hear about wrongful behavior. Wrong desires produce wrong behavior. They come from an inner desire to satisfy an unmet need that has existed in our life for a long time. For example, a person that has low self esteem will enter a bad relationship believing that by helping their partner, their own needs will be fulfilled. Or, someone that has a deep need to be loved by others might find himself or herself seeking the approval of peer groups, gangs and other unwholesome agents. In almost all cases, there are consequences from our efforts to satisfy our own neediness through wrongful behavior.

The resulting outcome may be behavior that is unacceptable to a normal society. When unmet needs remain unsatisfied, they may lead to wrong behavior from those unhealed. Wrong desires may lead to wrong marital relationships. Black children born out of these relationships are definitely more prone to end up with wrecked lives of their own. The escalating number of young black females and males deciding to have children outside of wedlock is another evidence of wrong desires. The constant search for destructive freedom will do nothing to give meaning to an empty life. But it will do everything to add additional unhealed hurts.

Unhealed hurts lead to more negative consequences. Low self-esteem causes us to nurse our unhealed hurts falsely. Does God really care about the wellness of Blacks? Let's look at what the scripture has to say to us. "The spirit of the Lord is upon me, because he hath anointed me to preach the gospel to the poor; he hath sent me to heal the broken hearted, to preach deliverance to the captives, and recovering of sight to the blind, to set at liberty them that are bruised" (Luke. 4:18).

Improper Life Choices

Whenever we have unresolved issues or thoughts about who we are, the consequences can be devastating. These issues may produce negative behavior patterns, bitterness, insecurities, indecisiveness, timidity, or excessive levels of aggressiveness. While growing up, such a person may never have adhered to the rules, known boundary limitations, or how to avoid wronging others. He may have grown up in a household where violence, cursing, and verbal abuse were acceptable behavior. Later in life, this upbringing will be challenged by a society that has certain norms and laws. If he never corrects these perceptions of lack of respect for rules and boundaries, he most likely will make unwise choices in life.

A black child might have no interest in studying because he has a low opinion and expectation of himself. Therefore, he finds it easier to resort to using physical strength to prove that he has value. His problem can usually be traced back to his formative years and the home he grew up in. It may have produced an attitude of self-reliance, self-justification, self-protection, self-centeredness, self-defense, etc. Thus, his wrong decisions and behavior is his way of gaining attention the only way he knows how. A stronghold of wrong attitudes, ideas, beliefs, motives, patterns and thinking becomes a part of his life experiences. Unless he receives healing support, his familiar experiences will lead him deeper into making wrong decision.

Increasing Rehabilitation Costs

There is a direct correlation between low self-esteem and expensive rehabilitation. The long-term negative effect of Blacks living emotionally and spiritually damaged is detrimental to all. Unless help is provided for those Blacks suffering with feelings of inadequacy and inferiority, the costs for rehabilitating or making them well will increase a financial burden on families and the nation as a whole. Therapeutic counseling and treatment programs are expensive. Emotional or physical handicaps always disable a portion of the available work force. The social and economic cost increases each time another black child or adult suffers from the social illness, "low self-esteem".

Long-term care cost for administering therapeutic counseling to black men incarcerated is astronomical. More detention facilities will be required to house the increasing prison population. And the great majority of the inmates are black. Welfare and family services cost to treat these inmates' families increases as well. Since low self-esteem does contribute significantly to prison and counseling crisis centers being overcrowded, every step that we take to prevent the damaged identity of the Black race is a success story.

From creation, low self-esteem and a poor self-image were not God's will for His people. Neither is it His will for us to be clueless regarding out true identity. To be plain, as a people, many of us have not yet grasped the plan of God for our lives. The Israelites were God's chosen people, but never really accepted the challenge to live sold out for God. As a result, they were sent into slavery. Blacks came out of a very similar slavery condition. Are we on our way back to slavery in the same way the Israelites were? What can Blacks as a race do to avoid self-destructing?

FIFTEEN

Stepping Out of the Black Identity Crisis

Acknowledge the Problem

A first step out of any problem is acknowledging you have one. Similarly, the Black race must admit they need help. During slavery, black slaves understood that it was not God's will for them to stay chained to the history of the past. Too many of Blacks do not acknowledge the crisis of Black America. Many see it as a phase that will pass.

A few slave leaders recognized the importance of their freedom, and got the help of their abolitionist Black and White supporters. There were some slaves who believed slavery was the only life because it provided them with a place to stay and food and shelter. But there were others who wanted to feel the sunshine of freedom and wanted to better themselves. It would not have done them any good to deny that they were wasting away on plantations.

There are many books that address Black America's social problems. But few actually get to the heart of the matter. Many wounds are self-inflicted. As a race, each of us must evaluate our own attitudes and diligence toward God. We must assume a part of the responsibility for our own problems and repent of sin and selfishness and begin to live for God.

More Christian-centered Training Required

A second step is more focus on Christian-centered training. According to the Word of God, the beginning of wisdom and understanding starts with knowledge of God.

Many black parents have never come to terms with the truth that they cannot raise God-fearing children if they themselves are not committed to obeying Him. God has given us everything that pertains to life and godliness. This does not mean that rearing children will be easy, but that the believer can be successful if he adheres to the standards and principle of God's living Word. Apostle Paul recorded for us, "I can do all things through Christ Jesus which strengthens me" (Philippians 4:13). This scripture offers real promise and hope for not only Afro Americans, but for all those who will take God at his word.

A few days ago I came across an article discussing contemporary training methods. The article suggested various options, but not one addressed the need for God. More money and more programs, alone, will not correct the problem that haunts Black America, nor our nation as a whole. Only raising responsible and accountable children will turn the tide of social ills.

Many parents have forgotten that family training is essential and that if they fail to follow through, their children will be lost forever, not only physically, but spiritually. Black parents work tirelessly to give their children material things they never had. Because of this, the children see this as the signal to expect more, to work less and to be irresponsible. Unless they hear a clear message that life is not about freebies, but about personal responsibility, they will grow into adulthood believing the world owes them something. And as we have seen, youth with these expectations take shortcuts to failure.

A few days ago I attended a school council forum that addressed poor school performance. The facilitator, who was obviously well informed on her subject, said the church needs to become involved in school discipline problems, which she identified as the number one hindrance to excellent school performance. The worst of these problem schools were predominantly black.

Although I knew there were problems in our schools, it appears that in some schools the problem is epidemic and not being addressed. Reports confirmed that many of the most qualified teachers are leaving the teaching field or transferring to schools where they can teach without hindrance. Diligent teachers are being badly attacked or abandoned by the very communities they have come to save.

Surprisingly, teachers see parents as hindrances in solving the discipline problem. They see themselves as victims of a system that won't protect them against undisciplined black children. Does anyone believe we do not have a black identity crisis in the schools? Only a return to solid values and discipline will turn the tide of chaos.

The Word of God tells us to train up children, not let them grow up according to their personal whims and desires. Material things can never replace godly training and discipline. Allowing a child to mature without proper guidance will ultimately lead him into lawlessness and disrespect for others. This is why prisons are full and overflowing. Criminal behavior does not begin in adulthood. In most cases, it can be traced back to defiance and rebellion that went unchecked in early years.

The Word of God was written to instruct man how to please God, and not to be selfish and self-seeking. Too many black parents see discipline as repressive and not corrective. Yet, God tells us that parents should use appropriate restraint to bring their children up in the reverence and admonition of the Lord. In many homes, secular training principles have replaced biblical principles as the preferred method of training.

Many black parents feel guilty for being so involved in their own pursuits. Thus, they relinquish effective spiritual discipline methods and make it up to their children with gifts. Others believe that religion is personal and do not believe in the Bible or God. This leads to their children becoming manipulative of both parents and the social system. The Word of God instructs us to do the opposite. "My son, despise not the chastening of the Lord; neither be weary of his corrections. For whom the Lord loves, he corrects; even as a father the son in whom he delights" (Proverbs 3:11-12). If black parents would listen and obey this wise instruction, we could contribute much to help change things in America.

Parents are not held responsible for choices made by grown children. But as parents, we must not disregard the tremendous responsibility we have in training and teaching them at early ages to follow after God. Unless parents train their children according to the Word of God, the children will eventually pay the price. The responsibility to train up the children belongs to the parents. Determination is a concept that we need to explain thoroughly to our children. It means to be completely focused on reaching your intended goal. Training and discipline are essential tools to accomplish one's purpose in life. Recently, the evening news reported an incident where a seventeen year old young black male went on a shooting spree wounding several other students. When a seventeen year old young man goes around shooting others, we have to ask ourselves "Are we failing our spiritual training mission?"

Know the Person God Has Ordained You to Become

A third step that will help us find our destiny is to get to know the person that God has called us to be. Most of us become either what we have decided we will be, or what others want us to be. The solution is to "stop trying to keep up with the Joneses." On numerous occasions, I have asked young and older Blacks, "Do you know who God has destined you to be?" In many instances, they are unsure because they really have spent no time seeking God's wisdom to determine their purpose in life.

Coming out of slavery, many Blacks went to the North and got caught in the quest for material goods. Acquiring things made them feel important. Going from slavery to freedom without supporting strong survival values, left them unable to cope with success.

The Apostle Paul had learned to be content with himself and his God. Paul declares, "Not that I speak in respect of want for I have learned to be content in whatever state I am" (Philippians 4:11). Paul learned that the person he was had nothing to do with what he owned, nor what others considered him to be. Here was a man who truly understood that he did not need to strive for mastery over things or people, because things will eventually burn. Further, he knew excellence in Christ was hindered by seeking things of the flesh. Therefore, he gladly counted all such things as waste, in comparison with the things of God.

Today, too many Blacks define themselves by personal and professional ownership. What we have yet to realize is that an abundance of material goods is not the same as the abundant life God offers. We are not to set our eyes upon things because they will become false gods. When a people's priority is God, they do not require things to give them value. When a race makes God its priority, it learns to be like Paul—rich in contentment.

Do you recall our discussion about black children choosing white dolls? Each child needs to know he is special to God, a one of a kind. They need to be taught to value the things Jesus values. When a person learns to love as Christ does, his identity is connected to the inner man, and not to external physical features. A contented person is someone who understands the beautiful person Christ has called him to be. He does not seek to become a carbon copy of someone else.

God does not desire a perfect man or woman, but one who will allow him to live out His life through them. Paul puts it this way: "I can do all things through Christ Jesus which strengthens me" (Philippians 4:13). He understood that he could only become great by allowing Christ to be Lord in every area of his life. This same Paul had at one time attempted to become great by murdering others. Therefore, he could gladly and boldly declare, "I am (now) what I am by the grace of God."

The trap of Satan is to dupe man into believing there are better solutions than those presented in the Word of God. But God is our only eternal refuge!

Yesterday, I received a frantic call from a black mother concerned about her daughter whose life was spiraling downward in the wrong direction. Before we could address her problem, she began to lose control and weep. For sixteen years she had trained her daughter to be a respectable Christian young lady. But now her daughter had rejected all she had been taught and was headed down the path of self-destruction.

This was a promising and highly intelligent young lady. She had confessed Christ and lived in a Christian home, dreaming of someday becoming a doctor. But something had gone wrong and she no longer had any interest in God. This mother was distraught and devastated. A day later I called the young lady to see how she was doing. During the conversation she shared with me that there was a young man in her life. It did not take much to figure out that she had made a critical mistake. She did not have to explain, because I knew what had occurred. She had become intimately involved with an ungodly older man. She had allowed him to become her priority, and he took advantage of the situation. He would purchase her gifts, and she gave her body to him. Before long, she had gotten deeper into a relationship that had little use for God. She is paying a great price for her decision to pursue pleasures over Christ. This man slid into a place that only God deserved. By allowing him to replace God, she also rejected her mother's training. What a tragedy when we do not know nor accept the person God has ordained us to become. The outcome is a person with a terribly misplaced value in him or herself.

A New Moral Conscience

A fourth step that will help Blacks in their struggle with significance is to reverse the present moral trend. This is not intended to convey that all Blacks have poor morals. I am saying that a people who once were very moral have become lax regarding the moral standards of a holy God. During slavery, Blacks were forced to become sexual and procreative vessels, but this was not by choice. Looking at contemporary America today, things have drastically changed. No one is being forced to sin against God, yet far too many Blacks live in sinful relationships outside of the will and Word of God.

They have reasoned that not even God should set moral standards for them.

As we discussed earlier much of this can be attributed to the entertainment world. Black celebrities are identified as great role models when in fact their lives are in disarray. Contemporary America is more concerned with stars and stardom than spirituality and positive values and strong morals. Sports heroes often cohabitate, and bear children out of wedlock and it appears that no one really cares as long as they perform well on stage.

Young Black America suffers from a lack of strong, morally excellent role models. There are some good role models, but they are most definitely not attractive to most of our youth. Because our youth are impressed with the fame and fortune Hollywood offers they see those things that pertain to godliness and holiness as boring and uninteresting. Without a doubt, the moral conscience of Black America is at a crossroad in history. The proper building blocks needed to restore the character and integrity of the Black race are often ignored as outdated and out of touch with contemporary society.

No matter how we look at it, we all need a proper moral compass to govern our behavior. We must sound the trumpet to warn that we are losing much of our rich and powerful Black heritage to negative influences. Affluence becomes a problem when a race forgets to hold fast to the God that bought them out of slavery. David said, "All my help comes from the Lord that made heaven and earth" (Psalm 121:2). It is good for us to know that our help comes from God and nowhere else. Otherwise we will rely on the things and people of this world to give us purpose and understanding. In the end, we will sink deeper into the depravity of sinfulness. God is the only avenue to true freedom and an eternal destiny.

Our ancestors were people that faced tremendous odds, but they sought God for answers. This generation searches for their solutions entirely apart from God. They conclude that they know what is best for them, when the Bible says the wide way leads to death. Through the soft and fuzzy message of freedom, deceit has fooled many of our people. They do not believe it is necessary to repent and obey God. Immorality and rebellion will not go unpunished, and these days few even know the difference between right and wrong anymore. Man has no hope of saving himself apart from God. In fact, only God can transform us, allowing us to fulfill our destiny as a people of excellence.

Years ago, Blacks may have been poor, but they had great respect for themselves and reverence for God. But with personal freedom, many forgot the importance of things like self-respect and dignity. Many young black females have no use for modesty or chastity.

Unfortunately, this attitude will attract those who seek to exploit the foolish. It has become fashionable to care only about appearance and not what is on the inside. It has become easy to discard values and principles for looks and pleasure, but such thinking leads to spiritual bankruptcy. Without a doubt, it is these flesh seeking practices that will prevent many Blacks from becoming children of God.

Tattoos have become the trend in identifying marks. Black women are as bad as men about tattooing their bodies. In the same way, too many young black men identify themselves with tattoos and earrings. Nothing is more disturbing than watch young men pursuing things that eventually will cloud their thinking and affect their judgment. Similar to the practice of wearing pants below one's buttocks, many Christian men and women pierce and tattoo themselves in an effort to find an identification mark that will make them feel special. In a sense this can also be an indication of an eroding value system. While they might believe that this has nothing to do with Christianity, it really does. Paul tells us the Christian should abstain from the appearance of evil because it can become a stumbling block to unbelievers.

By no means am I condemning those who adopt theses means to identify with the world. But I am concerned that these things will prevent them from understanding that they must seek a relationship with God and not the world to have a strong sense of significance. We are to be in the world, but not of the world. In essence, we must set godly standards, not participate in sin. The temptations of the world are many. As a race, Blacks must return to the principles that made them great. The decision to continue in the ways of the present world means that we are confused about our identity and destined to repeat our failures.

Instead of identifying with each other in sinfulness, Blacks need to encourage and strengthen those weak in faith to become stronger. It is disappointing to God when He invests so much into a people who push Him away instead of drawing near. His chosen people, Israel did the same thing. Let us not be like Israel whom God compared to a mule who refused to obey the voice of his master. Poor morality eventually destroys a people's ability to discern their end. When spiritual vision is lost, they no longer hear God's voice and they lose sight of who they were meant to be. They no longer walk and identify in the awareness and image God intended, but follow after strange man-made gods that will lead them toward eternal separation from God.

The Black Church Must Remain Faithful

A fifth essential change is to practice becoming a people determined to live by faith in God. This means much more than attending church on Sunday morning. In certain areas of the country many Blacks still attend church, but it means little if we aren't living according to righteousness and godliness. .

God has shown favor to the Black race, and in II Chronicles 7:16 He has given them a promise that if they are willing to turn from their ways to Him, He will bless them immeasurably. Far from the brush harbor make-do churches of yesterday, the black people have progressed. During slavery, they had to conceal their secret desire to know God. Today, no one can stop them from seeking the God of spirit and truth.

First, the church must become the true and living vessel of hope to Black America. There are churches on almost every corner in every city and town. Our communities have no shortage of brick and mortar church buildings, but a lack of committed people willing to be the church of the living God, who stand in faith. At the core of the Black identity crisis is *a lack of interest in God*. I am in no way stating that there are not some segments of black people serving God with all their hearts. But as a race, we have watered down the true gospel, and now tickle the churchgoer's ears. Many do not want to hear about Jesus Christ. Black children are growing up in homes that do not know, nor care to know the loving God of faith. Life begins with an understanding of who God is, through the person of Jesus Christ.

In the Bible, John tells us "He that hath the Son hath life, and he that hath not the Son hath not life" (I John 5:12). In other words, without Jesus Christ, there is no life, only death, hell and eternal separation from God. One can live a secular life here on earth, but it will be empty and full of false hope and despair. Ungodliness is a direct result of rebellion against God, going our own way. Yet, Jesus said, "I am the way, the truth and the life. No man cometh to the Father but by me" (John 14:6). And who should understand better than the church who Jesus Christ is? No other institution is capable of leading the world toward the truth other than the spirit-filled, living church of God. The family that turns to God will find love, forgiveness and restoration.

Our black ancestors might not have had the best education, but they understood that the key to living was in drawing closer to the Lord. While contemporary Blacks have progressed and accumulated much educational knowledge, wealth and fame, these things cannot save them from destruction. In fact, they can cause one to end up with a "mistaken identity." From the brush harbor churches, black slaves found a way to endure the degradation of slavery. But they received supernatural help from the same faithful God all Blacks need today. Families were torn apart, but God did not let the Black race become an extinct people. They heard the call of God. In II Chronicles 7:14 it says, "If my people called by my name will return to me...I will hear their cry and heal their land." We need to hear that call once again. Obedience and self-discipline are priceless principles of God.

While the problems of schools and our society are desperate, God has given us the means to address them by His Word. The church must take the lead, teaching the truth to those without understanding and wisdom. Failure to preach about sin will end in permanent separation from God.

Second, the church must teach and model behavior that is based upon the principles of scripture. For this reason the Apostle Paul instructed man "I beseech you therefore brethren, by the mercies of God that you present your bodies a living sacrifice, holy, acceptable unto God, which is your reasonable service. And be ye not conformed to this world, but be ye transformed by the renewing of your mind, that ye may prove what is that good and acceptable will of God" (Romans 12:1-2).

Scripture offers the wisdom of God and the means to overcome the Black struggle for identity. A person who thirsts after wisdom will find answers in Christ.

Romans 12:1-2 reminds us that we are human, and must have the divine help of the supernatural God to overcome the obstacles we face. The beginning of a transformed life starts and ends with repentance and salvation, getting to know God. The more we study the Word of God and get to know Him, the more we reflect the character of Christ. The Apostle Paul understood the urgency of developing the mind of Christ. Therefore, he advises us to become disciplined students of scripture. Discipline is a matter of the mind. It is not someone else's responsibility. Matthew 28:19-20 instructs the church to help people find Christ so they can get to know wisdom and knowledge. However, Philippians 2:5 instructs each person to come to Jesus so his thoughts can be wise.

Understanding the importance of the family unit in building positive self-confidence is vital to the future of Black America. In order to have strong families that know how to fulfill God's will and plan, the church must be alive and preaching Christ crucified.

When parents and their children are active and grounded in the living church of Jesus Christ, they will love to learn.

The unconditional love of God, offers hope to people in despair—hope for change, even total transformation. The church must be a model of unconditional love to help Blacks learn how to love themselves and others the way God loves them.

From the moment a baby is born, he needs parents and a church to teach him about his identity in Christ. The first place that a black child must learn to have a positive identity is in the home. Black parents often fail to help their children develop love and obedience to God. But children can't find their identity in Christ if their parents fail to attend church and seek God in their own lives.

Strong families are the foundation of black communities. The church offers the best hope of sustaining and reinforcing positive family values. Our churches need to be founded, grounded and rooted in the Word of God, and not in contemporary philosophies. A godly value system gives hope to those who feel insignificant, letting them know they were born with a purpose, to glorify the Lord Jesus Christ.

While the church has helped some with their identity issues, it has failed to reach a large segment of the population. This segment usually ends up in prison, on drugs, or dead. Why does this occur? Simply because these do not grasp whom they were meant to be. Because this internal struggle is invisible to the world, only those who live in the spirit will ever see the pain and emptiness of these people.

Jesus charged the church with the responsibility to make disciples, meaning they preached Christ and Him crucified as the only hope for lost mankind. Then in Mathew 28:18-20 He charged His church to take that saved person and make him a disciple. The church was purchased with His own shed blood. It is the mission of His church to encourage and help the lost find salvation, then take on the identity of Christ. It is to serve as a model of encouragement and reassurance, that God loves them and wants to transform their lives to reflect the character of Christ.

I was very pleased to learn that many churches have started literacy programs in an effort to help Blacks who cannot read. This will help them to feel a sense of achievement and significance. These efforts are being incorporated into the church worship and will help those Blacks with reading difficulties. Reading and studying the Bible will help them know God and understand their identity in Christ, forever changing their poor self-images.

One day when Jesus was out with his disciples, He asked them, "Who do people say the Son of Man is?" The disciples replied, "Some say John the Baptist; others say Elijah; and still others, Jeremiah or one of the prophets" (Matthew 16:13-14). But immediately Jesus asked his disciples, "But who do you say that I am?" Simon Peter answered, "You are the Christ, the Son of the living God" (Matthew 16:16). This verse is the key that unlocks the door of faith into the Kingdom of God. The church must embrace and teach Christ to those who have no relationship with the living Son of God. When Jesus becomes real, a person is transformed. A dead church cannot usher in the presence or power of the resurrected Christ. Neither can it develop the godly character and image that He requires.

So what must the church offer a lost world? It must offer the preaching of Christ and Him crucified. Nothing else will change hearts like the pure, unadulterated gospel of Christ. Nothing Jesus touches is ever the same again. Thus, if the contemporary church wants to be ready when He returns, it must dump everything that does not glorify God and get back to the basics of loving and serving God, sacrificing self and rejecting sin.

I find it very interesting that God chose to live in us in the person of the Holy Spirit. The new believer actually houses the Holy Spirit of God who refines and raises us, transforming us from death to life. Christ came that He might experience all the like temptations of man such as suffering, emptiness, rejection and isolation. He also wanted to help man experience joy, belonging, friendship, love and a deep grasp of truth.

When the church demonstrates this personality and new character of Jesus Christ, it too learns to become a beacon that shines with the love of Christ, building godly character and strong identity.

Jesus demonstrated the importance of being a servant to bring about spiritual changes. The Apostle Paul said that Jesus, "being in the very nature with God, did not consider equality with God something to boast about, but made himself nothing, taking on the very nature of a servant, being made in human likeness. And being found in the appearance of a man, he humbled himself and became obedient to death--even death on the cross" (Philippians 2:6-8). And because He chose to humble Himself on our behalf, God set Him on His right hand in heaven.

There is a dynamic spiritual revelation for Blacks to grasp from the servant hood of Jesus. Christ gave up His place in heaven to die as a sacrifice for sinful men. He modeled for us the eternal image of our glorious God. To regain its true identity as the Bride of Christ, Blacks must be willing to take their rightful place as servants of Christ. The church must instruct men and women how to become servants, living not for themselves but for Christ. Believers must reflect the character of Jesus without regard to the color of someone's skin.

Consequently, Christian parents must once again set aside their own desires as a sacrifice for the good of their children. The world must be introduced to a sanctuary of servants, and not exalted cliques with agendas of their own. Instead of looking for stars, the living church of God must recruit disciples that will lay down their lives to serve Christ.

Now is the time for the church to stop exalting money and things and get back to the basics of worshiping in spirit and in truth, serving the Lord with our whole hearts. Loving and obeying God is the benchmark of the true church of Christ.

Too many churches have become entangled with the rudiments and traditions of the world. In order to project the image of the resurrected Christ, His church must examine itself. It is time for the church to diligently evaluate whether it is a life-changing vessel of Jesus Christ.

Speaking as a Black American, I believe the Black race has misidentified its place and purpose in society. Obedience to the will of God usually takes a back stage seat to our programs, professional and academic accomplishments, salaries and stages. The humility of Jesus is something each believer should strongly desire. Our worship is dying for lack of it. As a race, we could do with more faithful black pastors, preachers, and congregations. In order to lead the way for unsaved folks, those who proclaim an identity as vessels of Jesus Christ, ought to practice what they preach. Thus, Jesus declared, "If you love me, keep my commandments" (John 14:15).

In John 14:15, the believer is instructed to keep Jesus' words and live in obedience, which will guarantee the believer a position in life as well as intimacy with the person of Christ. The person who obeys Christ becomes more than a professor of the new message, but a possessor of the Kingdom of God. When the church fulfills its role as the teacher of kingdom principles, those who enter a new relationship with Jesus will also possess His spiritual identity as a new creation. Temporal values and things will fade in significance, and have less influence in shaping our lives. When Jesus rules supreme, love for the things of the world ceases.

Presently, too many black worship centers practice religion instead of preaching Christ. Christianity is the business of the church, not money and man-made programs. Earlier churches use to emphasize obedience and self-sacrifice. The message of the early church was the resurrected Christ. Contemporary worship must emphasize the love of Jesus and obedience, so that the unsaved are introduced to the life-changing gospel. Through his power they will find strength and a new personal identity. What the world needs to see is a living church seeking a deeper insight into the person of Jesus Christ.

Third, the church must become a true witness, and focus on preaching an eternal kingdom theology. In other words, it must become real. Lately, it seems that not a day goes by that someone does not demand that the church be revived to be an effective agent for change.

God's purpose for His church is that it glorifies Him and leads others to know Him. Satan is always looking to transform people into his cheap, sinful image. In Luke 4:3 he even tried to persuade Jesus to doubt his own divinity and disobey God.

Young people today need a transformed church that conforms to the identity of Christ. This is especially true for those young troubled black youths searching for an individual identity that will provide them with assurance that they are somebody special.

When Satan tempted Jesus he underestimated His eternal commitment. Unaware that Jesus had humbled Himself, Satan foolishly tempted Him with temporal powers and material wealth. But Jesus had no need for anything Satan offered him, and neither do we. He already knew His exalted position was with the Father in the Kingdom. So why did He have any need of Satan's temporal things? To help change the skewed identity of black people, Christ must be exalted as the God of truth and life. After all he said, "If I be lifted up, I will draw all men unto me." In Philippians 2:8 the Apostle Paul marveled at the faithfulness of Christ and his humility. Paul's character was transformed by the eternal vision and power of the Holy Spirit. From then on, he had no reason to ever seek his identity through temptation and self-centeredness.

Fourth, the church is God's agent for spiritual restoration. Black America suffers from the need to be restored to the image and awareness of its Creator, God. The church must serve as witness to the truth of the gospel. If it does not live up to its calling, then the world will suffer also for lack of living examples to confirm the truth of God's holy Word. When the church is true to its witness, mouths will be stopped who say the church is full of hypocrites. For this reason, the Apostle Paul devoted his life to spreading and preaching the good news of the gospel. The Bride of Christ, the church must demonstrate honesty, sincerity, love, forgiveness, compassion, and faith. If Christ came to give Himself a ransom for the lost, so must His witness, the church. When people are swept away after worldliness and ungodliness, the church must be a powerful beacon of truth and light. A redeemed church offers the only hope for life's problems. And who is that solution? Jesus Christ! Both inside and outside of churches, people do not know who they were meant to be. When they come to know Christ and the life-changing power of his resurrection, they have the foundation necessary to overcome low self-esteem and identity confusion. Being restored and assured of one's identity will empower them to encourage others weak in faith. Galatians 6:1 says the spiritual person should restore those that are weak.

Fifth, when the church understands its mission and purpose it will understand that it has been called to be a bold witness to evangelize the world. Our churches need to become bold witnesses for Christ. Their testimony should affirm their confidence in the living Christ. This boldness will serve as proof of the transforming power of Christ to defeat the enemy and his deceptions. The church must present Him as the answer to the evils of our present evil world.

The hip-hop world and entertainment industries are bold for Satan. But is the church bold for Christ? Too few Christians are sold out and willing to exalt Christ as the head of their lives. We must not confuse exalting Him with just attending church on Sunday morning. But, will we be a living sacrifice, laying down our agenda for His? The Apostle Paul said, "We should fix our eyes on Jesus as the author and finisher of our faith, who for the joy set before him endured the cross, scorning the shame, and sat down at the right hand of the throne of God. Consider him who endured such opposition from sinful men, so that you will not grow weary and lose heart" (Hebrews 12:2-3).

The church must teach and train those weak in faith that evil cannot win out over faith. It must be firmly established on the principles of scripture. Further, this faith must denounce worldliness as an alternative to the pure and undefiled gospel of Jesus Christ. Too often, the black church crosses that demarcation line that should separate the world from the Bride of Christ. Consequently, it is becoming more difficult to convince unbelievers that the church has a message worth considering.

To be effective in changing the world, the church needs to be respected, set apart for God. The church must be loyal to Him and His mission. Our contemporary churches have many public personalities but most lack solid commitment. Many fail to model a living Christian faith. Sunday is the busiest day of the week for church attendance. It is also a day that folks come into the church to hear the Word of God, experience spiritual change, and exit to live out the gospel of Christ.

Matthew 28:19-20 says Christ expects His church to be loyal to His charge. What makes it so difficult to be loyal to God? It is a direct result of our selfish nature. The local church is not to be a selfish institution. The world watches those who profess to know and love God. When the church lives for God with fire and passion, the world will stand up and take notice. They'll be intrigued with the idea of a living God who involves Himself in the affairs of men.

Selfishness has pervaded the church in exactly the same way it has the world. The church must do as the Apostle Paul instructed in Colossians 3:5 and "Mortify the flesh." This means that those who profess to know Christ and His changing power must mortify their selfish desires, putting God first. Too many professing Christians operate out of their old man and not out of the power of the Spirit. Jesus declared, "For whoever wants to save his life will lose it, but whoever loses his life for me will find it" (Matthew 16:25). What message should this send to the black person struggling to hang onto that uncommitted life? It should prompt him to realize that he must die to self and live unto the character and destiny planned by Christ.

Before being born again we live unfulfilled, empty lives that center around us and what we want. After coming to Christ we should begin to resemble the character of Christ. Unfortunately too many Blacks continue to conform to the image of a world system that is anti-Christian. Furthermore, many of our worship centers hold services that do not charge the congregation to mortify worldly behavior and habits. As a sanctuary of the Holy Spirit, Christians must demonstrate their loyalty to Him by living a life that is different and distinctively unique. Loyalty must not be a mere word, but must be walked out in righteousness and holiness. The church must model life to a lost world.

A sixth step the church must take is a life of integrity. Unless black leaders and congregants realize the church has lost its salt, they will continue to travel the path of double-mindedness. James identified this as one looking in the mirror and walking away, ignoring what he sees. When a nation loses much of its personal integrity, its identity will be lost. It is the church who must hold up the standard of righteousness that imparts significance.

When the church loses its salt, it damages the reputation of Christians. Many Blacks have rebelled against God and the laws of man. Having no conviction against it, they begin living for themselves, with only a vague, shallow sense of godliness, a fraud.

When this occurs, the integrity of the church is put on the line. At this point the church is impotent and empty. Because of a decline in the integrity in today's church, it has lost credibility in a world that needs to see the real thing. Leaders and lay members are often little more than pretentious and insincere professors of a faith that they are powerless to live out. The integrity of pastors and church officials is questioned more today.

As Christians, we are to be branches attached to the Vine, Christ Jesus, and if we don't have His life flowing through us, we are dead and have nothing to offer anyone. We dare not let the fire of the spirit go out, but stir it up within us, reflecting Christ in all we do.

Throughout history, the church has been a beacon of hope, a promise of transformation and eternal life. Jesus Himself constantly accused the Pharisees and clerical leaders of being little more than hypocrites. And why did He do that? He did that because they were only concerned with their own prestige, and not with needs of others. As in the past, it is paramount that the church be seen as a compassionate and consistent place of hope and promise. To those who are faint and have no hope, it is the local churches and pastoral leaders who should lead the way.

We often hear the expression: "It's time to stop playing church." How true this slogan is. When the church is a playhouse instead of a prayer house, the results are disappointing. Church leaders cannot make people live a life of integrity. But they can demonstrate their personal convictions and walk holy of the vocation whereby they have been called.

When people don't really know who they are in Christ, they are prone to take on the character and behavior that contradicts the will of God. The Pharisees did not believe or understand who Jesus was because they did not comprehend the will of God. They knew about God, but did not belong to Him. Their actions were a direct result of pretending to possess an intimate relationship with God, but their lives were not transformed. There is no darkness in Jesus Christ.

Thus, the living church of Christ must be a vessel of hope and light to those without hope and on the verge of fainting. Our refusal to come clean with God and remain hypocritical will erode the credibility of the church to those who need a guiding light.

A resistant to teach and preach God's Word and truth has produced generations of people who remain unchanged, without godliness and righteousness. Leaving God out of the equation will lead to chaos and hopelessness. Maybe we have not yet reached our lowest point, but if Black America does not take responsibility for its own failure to obey God, we are definitely destined to repeat our past mistakes. Freedom means responsibility both inside and outside the church.

Historically, the church has been slow to carry out the mandate of the gospel as instructed in Matthew 28:18-20.

As a result, it is often seen by the world as a sanctuary in disarray. This has prompted many to raise the question: Is the church of Black America (1) predominantly after money to pay expensive salaries, (2) a place not calling for spiritual unity, (3) a refuge that unsaved people can come to for handouts, (4) uninterested in changing lives and not conformed to the image of Jesus, and (5) a sanctuary used for singing?

Because of such doubt raised about the sincerity of the church, it is essential that each Christian be determined to help others get to know the real Jesus Christ. Apostle Paul said, "We then that are strong ought to bear the infirmities of those weak in faith" (Romans 15:1).

Recently, I discussed with another believer the need for a truly universal church revival. We agreed that Christ instructed His church to take care of the widows and poor, and give hope to those lost without Him. Without the proper leadership from the church, people easily adopt a worldly philosophy. They adapt to the image of the world and not God. Today, we are witnessing a race of people that struggles with their identity. The church is at that pivotal point in history to rise up and help show them the way.

In the Book of Ecclesiastes, Solomon declares that the whole duty of man is to fear God and to obey His words.

In a day when Blacks desperately needs God, too many believers are remaining silent. We seem to have no advice to give to those seeking answers. God has no respect of color, creed or gender. His love crosses all boundaries. Therefore, it is time that the living church must live for Christ as never before.

God will not accept meager excuses for our failures when He comes again. He will seek for a pure Bride, set free from both physical and spiritual bondage through the person of Jesus Christ. Upon his return Christ will look for his saved church made up of all races, kindred and nations. Blacks are expected to be there to celebrate him in great numbers.

Conclusion

Is there hope for the black race? There is hope in the person of Jesus Christ for everyone who will accept his unconditional love and plan of salvation. God wants to draw near and be intimate with black people. Thus it is vital that we preach Christ. Black families and the church community must rise to the call for revival, being set apart to live for Christ as never before. Jesus is in the business of healing those suffering from low self-esteem

There is no single answer for all the problems confronting black people. But in Christ, Blacks can find significance and a reason to live. After trying everything else, converted Blacks have found that Jesus is the answer to every question.

If the church lives out its mandate, people will see the power and love of God in action.

Jesus challenges each believer to deny himself, take up his cross and follow Him. He is the only one worth following, the only source of life. The key to self-confidence is the assurance that God loves us and that He will use us to glorify the name of Jesus Christ. Black parents can model a passion for Christ that will transform the lives of their children and save them from eternal separation from God.

I personally would like to offer fifteen steps that will help anyone who seeks a spirit-filled life. These steps have been a tremendous blessing in my own personal journey with God.

1. Be honest with yourself and God, and be sure you have a personal relationship with Christ. (John 15: 10-12)

2. Commit yourself to God according to his Holy Word that is able to make you wise in all things. (Luke 1:74)
3. Make up your mind to start tithing because it is financial planning at its best. (II Corinthians 9:6-8)
4. Develop the proper attitude toward worshiping God. (John 4:24)
5. Put God first in everything. (Micah 6:8)
6. Remove the clutter/junk from your life. (Romans 12:1, 2)
7. Develop your ability to love and forgive others so God will forgive you. (I Corinthians 13, Galatians 5:13-15)
8. Learn to laugh a lot and be grateful, and do not complain. (Proverbs 17:22; I Timothy 6:6)
9. Become consistent in your prayer and devotional life. (II Timothy 2:7; James 5:13-18)
10. Trust in God with all your heart, mind, and soul. (Psalm 46:1-2, Proverbs 3:5)
11. Develop an aggressive faith. (Philippians 1:20-21; 4:13)
12. Die to yourself daily. (James 4:7; Ephesians 4:24)
13. Become a better witness for Jesus Christ. (II Corinthians 5:20; Matthew 28:19-20)
14. Learn to walk in the purpose of God for your life. (Ephesians 1:11; II Corinthians 13:5)
15. Set your sights toward eternity. (Philippians 3:12-14, Psalm 144:15)

While these steps might seem much too simple, I strongly encourage you to try them and see how different you feel about yourself. Our ancestors did not necessarily have these fifteen steps to overcome the scars left by slavery, but they too received revelation knowledge from God regarding how to leave past hurts behind. In turn, they received strength in the resurrection power of God. A favorite thought of mine is "No one knows what lies ahead, but if he holds onto the past he will never know what his future holds."

No matter what your heartache is, let God touch the pain. If you trust God and His healing power to love and exhort you to walk and live out your destiny, you will no longer feel insignificant or need external things to define who you are. When God blew His breath into us, we became His living soul.

Because God's opinion is the only one that matters, we must please Him. And when we come to the end of life's journey, He will ask us, "What did you do with the identity I gave you?"

No matter what race one belongs to, you are special, designed in His image, born with a purpose that God has ordained for you. We do not discover our purpose in someone else's shadow. We find significance when we **"comprehend the meaning and joy of life through Jesus Christ."** We must not be content to be defined by the opinions of men or worldly success. Those with a strong identity, like the Apostle Paul, count themselves to be nothing apart from an intimate relationship with Jesus Christ.

Having the proper self-identity will cause a person to change his direction to follow after the Word of God. Paul had a confused identity before becoming a disciple of Jesus Christ. But Romans 12:1-2 says when he accepted Christ, he became transformed. Therefore he could boldly declare, "But what things were gain to me, those I counted loss for Christ" (Philippians 3:7). Philippians 4:13, 19 tell us he no longer depended on man to determine his purpose and this life, or the life to come.

We are living in a contemporary world that cares little for the things of God, and yet He is the only one who can enable us to fulfill our purpose. In general, the world is a threshold for people in hot pursuit of a life separate from the will and plan of God. It is easy to become drawn to things that bring temporary pleasure. But the love for these things leads to destruction. The Apostle Paul knew this and separated himself from everything and everyone that would cause him to question his identity.

God says we are each special, made in His image, significant. For years I have urged others to stop accepting what others think and say about them, and instead seek God's plan.

Just how much does your identity mean to Jesus? Listen to the question He posed to His disciples: "Who do people say the Son of man is?" They replied: "Some folks believe you to be John the Baptist; others think that you are Elijah, or Jeremiah, or one of the prophets" (Matthew 16:13-14). Was Jesus unaware of the answer? Of course he knew what the town people thought.

But as we saw earlier, Jesus was not really interested in what others thought. He was interested in who the disciples thought He was, based on their relationship. After all, these were those closest to him. It was imperative that they know His character and purpose. Otherwise, they would not know their own identity. And if they didn't, they would be poor and ineffective witnesses. In order to bring others to know him, they had to be sure of Him and themselves. Jesus considered His identity critical to His mission.

Subsequent to that conversation, Peter finally grasped the point—that Jesus was Messiah. Jesus responded, "Blessed are thou, Simon Barjona: for flesh and blood hath not revealed it unto thee, but my father which is in heaven"

(Matthew 16:17). Jesus knew that Peter would have to be sure of who He was in order to handle ministry. By correctly identifying who Jesus was, Peter confirms that he was in right relationship with God or else he would not have been able to answer that question. And once Peter understood who Jesus was, he could be sure of his own identity.

I want to share a Bible verse that will help those who are caught up in material things, money, sex, and power. Those things will never make you a spiritually confident person. But the following verse will.

In the last few years I've come to understand what the Apostle Paul meant when he said, "We are his workmanship, created in Christ Jesus for good works, which God prepared beforehand that we should walk in them" (Ephesians 2:10). When we are born again we are remade in His image. It's incredible to know that God gave His Son, Jesus Christ, as a sacrifice so we could have His image. True contentment is accepting the person that we were meant to be in Christ Jesus. We can never be better than that. The world is a counterfeit reflection of the glorious image of Christ. Your identity is not dependent upon others, but upon your acceptance of the wonderful person God has destined you to be. It is up to you to accept His salvation and His definition of success.

The world's system cannot guarantee your freedom, but God can. In His arms we can rediscover our misplaced identity. Has your identity been misplaced or stolen? If you allow Jesus to reveal Himself to you, you will never be the same again.

Printed in the United States
104105LV00002B/166-435/P